Research Guide to Japanese Film Studies

Michigan Monograph Series in Japanese Studies
Number 65

Center for Japanese Studies
The University of Michigan

Research Guide to Japanese Film Studies

Abé Mark Nornes
and
Aaron Gerow

Center for Japanese Studies
The University of Michigan
Ann Arbor, 2009

Published by the Center for Japanese Studies,
The University of Michigan
1007 E. Huron St.
Ann Arbor, MI 48104-1690

Library of Congress Cataloging in Publication Data

Nornes, Markus.
Research guide to Japanese film studies / Abé Mark Nornes and Aaron Gerow.
p. cm. — (Michigan monograph series in Japanese studies ; no 65)
Includes bibliographical references and indexes.
ISBN 978-1-929280-53-7 (cloth : alk. paper) — ISBN 978-1-929280-54-4 (pbk. : alk. paper)
1. Motion pictures—Japan. 2. Motion picture industry—Japan. 3. Film archives—Directories. 4. Motion picture film collections—Directories. 5. Motion pictures—Japan—Bibliography. I. Gerow, Aaron. II. Title. III. Series.

PN1993.5.J3N67 2009
791.430952--dc22

2009000666

This book was set in Palatino Macron.
Kanji set in Hiragino Mincho Pro W3.

This publication meets the ANSI/NISO Standards for Permanence of Paper for Publications and Documents in Libraries and Archives (Z39.48—1992).

Printed in the United States of America

To Makino Mamoru
Our bibliographic *shishō*

Contents

Acknowledgments

This book was made possible by the generous help from the Center for Japanese Studies at the University of Michigan and its publication program as well as Harvard University's Reischauer Institute of Japanese Studies. An early draft was perused by a number of our colleagues: Roland Domenig, Fujiki Hideaki, Stuart Galbraith IV, Chika Kinoshita, Thomas Lamarre, Daisuke Miyao, Mitsuyo Wada-Marciano, Naoki Yamamoto, and Mitsuhiro Yoshimoto. Their comments certainly made this a better book. In our attempt to cover all the bases, a number of people kindly shared their expertise in areas we had yet to explore. They include Roger Macy, Kyoko Hirano, Satō Yō and Jennifer Robertson.

Finally, many archivists and bibliographers around the world provided the latest information on their collections and the ins and outs of using them. They include Rika Iezumi Hiro (Getty Research Center), Mona Nagai and Jason Sanders (Pacific Film Archive), Kenji Niki and Shevon Desai (University of Michigan), Satō Atsuko, Hiruta Mari and Suzuki Marie (Japan Foundation), Tabatake Kiyoko (Ikeda Bunko), Usui Michiko (Waseda University), Josie Walters-Johnston (Library of Congress), Sébastien Bondetti (Cinémateque français), Moriwaki Kiyotaka (Museum of Kyoto), Charles Silver (MOMA), Amy Heinrich (Columbia University), Harco Gijsbers (Netherlands War Documentation Institute), Kazuko Sakaguchi (Harvard University), Sotogawa Toyoko (Yamanashi Prefectural Library), Sunaoshi Hisao (Education Library), Zhao Jing (China Film Archive), Nico de Klerk and Francesco Izzo (Netherlands Filmmuseum), Mika Lawler (National Diet Library), Maureen Donovan (Ohio State University), Wong Ain-ling (Hong Kong Film Archive), Itō Tomoko (Toyota Kyōdo Shiryōkan), Teresa Silk (Imperial War Museum), Ellen Hammond and Haruko Nakamura (Yale University), Tochigi Akira, Okada Hidenori, and Irie Yoshirō (National Film Center), Watsuki Ayumi and Hamazaki Yoshiharu (Kawasaki City Museum), and Wachi Yukiko (Kawakita Memorial Film Institute).

We want to add you, the reader, to this list! Is there a source, new or old, that you feel should have made the cut? Have you stumbled across an archive that we should know about? Did you find mistakes? Please tell us. We hope to issue updated editions of this book, and any and all suggestions are welcome. Even better, use our book and write something new that we can write up the next time around!

Introduction

by Aaron Gerow

Research on Japanese cinema has always been an uphill climb.

The first studies in Japan were written before 1920 and were faced with social prejudices that, fueled by the hysteria over the popularity of crime films like *Zigomar*, viewed the movies as vulgar entertainment or, worse, the source of cultural or moral degradation. With the playing field so defined, film study either played along, attempting to confirm these opinions, or valiantly tried to defend the cinema (although sometimes by only confirming dominant values). In either case, studies of cinema were accorded at best secondary importance, often reduced by official culture to the same level in the cultural hierarchy as film itself. With the exception of Nihon and Waseda universities, which sported early film study programs, academia largely ignored the discipline and even today offers few opportunities for scholars. This has affected the quality of much research. Most film books in Japan are still published without footnotes and extensive bibliographies or filmographies, and, caught in the intellectual culture industry of publish, publish, publish, some of the more popular film scholars spend little time checking their facts or information.

Even if Japanese cinema rose in status during and after WWII as a means of promoting national images at home and abroad, film production and research garnered little support. As was clear with the system of designating important cultural properties, Japanese culture was often defined as what came before Westernized modernity, which left Japanese cinema the ironic problem of being insufficiently Japanese to be worthy of support or research. Such attitudes have unfortunately shaped the research environment for film, and this guide is in many ways both a historical description of these difficult conditions and a map for navigating them.

For instance, the major periodical index, the Diet Library's *Zasshi kiji sakuin*, first largely ignored film magazines. When it did begin including them, it only picked a few and indexed them in ways that were hard to use (not indexing film reviews, for instance). Only recently has the index expanded its coverage of film magazines and begun to fill in the decades long gaps. Film archives were also founded late in Japan and were mostly focused on preserving film, not facilitating research. Scholars used to the openness of foreign film collections will quickly notice the cold, bureaucratic, and often "user-unfriendly" attitudes of Japanese archives and libraries. Most institutions have improved in recent years due to bureaucratic reforms and the revival of the Japanese film industry, but the official emphasis on film as a business, not as a culture or an academic discipline, has placed archives in a weak position with regard to film companies. Even if a film or a still is clearly in the public domain, many archives will balk at letting you have images without permission if the company is still in existence, for fear of rubbing those companies in the wrong way.

The obstacles are not any lower when studying Japanese film abroad. Even if film study, if not also cinema in general, has been better recognized in countries like the United States, it long carried a hubris that, if not privileging Western cinema as the center of film practice, at least pretended the "distant observer" of non-Western cinemas like Japan had complete access to the cinematicity of the works, and thus did not need to engage with the complex local intertextuality of non-Western films. Film archives did collect Japanese movies, sometimes sooner and better than Japanese libraries, but they did not pursue the same kind of thorough collection of associated materials (books, magazines, ephemera, etc.) and creation of filmographies, bibliographies and indexes that they did for Western film. The cataloging of Japanese films at the Library of Congress in the United States—one of the most significant collections outside of Japan—was so poor in terms of transliterations and filmographic accuracy that it was often hard to figure what film a catalog record was referring to. Major indexes like the *FIAF International Index to Film Periodicals* do not include a single Japanese language periodical. At one level this is the responsibility of the FIAF members in Japan (and a Japanese government that underfunds those archives), but it also reflects an attitude on the part of the discipline in the West that pays insufficient attention to inequalities in film studies resources on an international scale. In the end, Western film studies often defines cinema as what it can study in its languages and relegates much of the hard research on non-Western cinema—except what it can appropriate—to the realm of area studies.

Unfortunately, area studies has also undervalued cinema studies. Japan scholars abroad have long ignored modern popular culture, either echoing Japanese official definitions of culture, or pursuing orientalist visions of culture that freeze Japan in a timeless past. Such major indexes as Naomi Fukuda's *Bibliography of Reference Works for Japanese Studies* privileged literature, history and the high arts at the expense of the vast amount written on film, especially in Japanese, and university libraries refused to collect such film-related materials as magazines. Top institutions like Yale and Michigan had perhaps a shelf's worth of film books in Japanese up until a few years ago, while also possessing twice that many volumes on obscure novelists that most people have forgotten. The situation has vastly improved at some of the major libraries, but only if they have the money and commitment. There remain colossal gaps to fill, ones both geographic and material.

It is important to know of such obstacles and the history behind them in part because the age of digital information sometimes gives us the illusion that such barriers are gone and accurate data is only a few keystrokes away. Perhaps this will become the case in the future, but it is definitely not true now when it comes to Japanese cinema. Although online databases like the Internet Movie Database (IMDB, 151) have provided convenient links to reviews and other useful material, basic data on the film or individual is often incomplete and not always accurate. While sites like the IMDB or Wikipedia ideally become accurate through cross-checking, as others correct someone's mistakes, the global flows of information management are unequal and data on non-Western cinema on such sites is notoriously sparse and inadequately vetted.

Even Japanese databases can suffer from these problems. User-managed sites are warped by fashion, such that certain recent popular movies have inordinately long entries while historically central, yet not currently trendy works are given scant attention. Those created by institutions are often restricted by lack of money or effort. Thus the online *Kinema junpō* database does not include prewar films, and its name readings are not always reliable. It is quite symbolic of conditions that the most comprehensive Japanese-language internet tool for cinema, the Japanese Movie Database (152), was compiled largely by one person, and thus, while a godsend to many, has mistakes and depends on the whims of that individual (the database, in fact, has become largely dormant as that person has abandoned updating it). This is not a critique leveled solely at online or digital resources; one can see similar problems with many print materials, in English or in Japanese. Japanese cinema studies has enjoyed neither the support nor the recognition that could have helped fund the production of a range of rigorous printed reference books and study facilities necessary to pursue the field.

For better or for worse, these obstacles are so fundamental that they influence the definition of the discipline of Japanese film studies itself. As mentioned above, it was articulations of cinema in Japan and abroad that shaped these obstacles, just as it was the unique problems that cinema seemingly posed to authorities in Japan or Japan scholars in America that prompted reactions that often exacerbated, not solved, these hurdles. What we do as scholars or students of Japanese cinema is to an extent determined by the unique overlapping of these influences. Thus, while it is ideal to question disciplinary boundaries that artificially impose ideologies of knowledge—Japanese film studies has suffered much from this and is thus one discipline, as Mitsuhiro Yoshimoto has argued in his book on Kurosawa Akira, that can uniquely challenge the academy—Japanese film has developed in particular conditions that require particular forms of research. That makes it difficult for anyone to just suddenly start researching the subject.

In some cases, this can mean having to learn Japanese. It is encouraging to see the publication of a number of English-language reference works, such as Alexander Jacoby's dictionary of directors (93), which provide reliable information that can benefit researchers who know little Japanese. Too many previous works, like the Weisser dictionaries, contained enough mistakes to render them difficult to use for serious research. Yet there are simply not enough reference works available in English to perform any extensive research. Even with the general paucity of authoritative materials, there is far more available in Japanese. That said, those who have not completely mastered the language can greatly benefit from resources that provide, for instance, name readings, filmographies or even stills.

All of these factors may shape and define our discipline, but they do not prevent the strategic use of and negotiation with present conditions. We are faced with an uneven playing field, but one that is also not too strictly regulated; it in fact offers exciting opportunities to the degree it is not fully shaped. With all the obstacles that exist, Japanese film studies, more so than with research on major Western cinema, demands that the scholar build up a research foundation partially on his or her own, by bearing considerable responsibility to verify fundamental information, cooperate with fellow scholars, and mutually raise the level of research to a high standard. He or she cannot simply work alone and rely on a single source for information. Yet that also means the researcher can be like the *bricoleur*, using a variety of skills and knowledges transcending any one field to strategically combine, collaborate, and construct.

There is in fact no solitary authoritative source of knowledge in the discipline. The Kinema Junpōsha dictionaries, for instance, may be one of the best sources for director and actor name readings, biographies and filmographies, but there are mistakes (Suwa Nobuhiro's name, for instance, is rendered "Suwa Atsuhiko" in the 1997 edition of the director dictionary). The National Diet Library, usually the authoritative source for name readings, may get Suwa's name right, but it gets Ushihara Kiyohiko's wrong (rendering it "Kyohiko") and rarely provides name readings for filmmakers beyond the director and screenwriter. It is incumbent upon the researcher to consult multiple resources so as to verify basic information. Frankly, it is hard climbing up the hill of Japanese film studies, and unfortunately, there are too many researchers who do not take the time and the effort to do this. The result is that there are otherwise fine discussions of Japanese cinema that are marred by elementary errors. These only damage the field as unsuspecting readers then use that mistaken information as fact, and spread it.

The lack of resources, however, has also left space for creative production of resources and greater collaboration between scholars. One of the consequences of the difficulties of Japanese film studies has been the development of cooperative ventures to share the burden of study and the information obtained. While some scholarly spaces still operate in an old version of the esoteric teacher-disciple relation, where both knowledge and the means of obtaining it were passed on as if in secret, a project like Kinema

Club, which started out as a group of young Japanese film scholars who shared copies of tables of contents of old journals, has been innovative and quite public, even if it has been hampered by lack of funding. Those of us involved have always hoped it could serve as an original model not only for studying Japanese film, but also of pursuing research on cinema or Japan—of what an academic discipline could be like.

This guide is in many ways a continuation of the Kinema Club project. We in fact started this book separately, I focusing on bibliography and Markus trying to cast a wider web. We could have refused to cooperate in order to each obtain the sole credit thought necessary to get promoted in American academia; we could have even abandoned the project in order to monopolize the resources and knowledge that many in the Japanese research world keep secret so as to maintain their authority. Instead, the two of us chose to pool our different resources, and the resulting work has benefitted enormously from that decision.

Our aim is to create, not just a survival guide to help students and scholars navigate the obstacles of Japanese film study, but also a program for changing the conditions and in some ways the meaning of study. We hope to alter the definition of the field, not from the top down, declaring the canonical works that everyone must read, but from the bottom up, encouraging all of us who love Japanese movies to put that affection and enthusiasm into a careful and concerted approach to the medium that, precisely because it can crystallize a collective effort, can budge even the heaviest obstacles. Following Yoshimoto, we strongly believe that the study of Japanese cinema can help alter the definitions of culture, academia, and scholarly disciplines, in part because research on Japanese film has often been excluded from these institutions due to the threat it poses to their established ideologies. But this is not simply a theoretical problem. Research on Japanese cinema must ultimately be defined on the ground through practice, through our own disgruntled resistance to the conditions forced upon us. The more of us, the better, for it is only the critical weight of our cooperative effort that can change such poor conditions and help us all move up the sometimes exasperating hill of Japanese cinema study.

A Guide to Using This Guide

This guide is the first of its kind in the field of Japanese film studies and is rare in both cinema, scholarship, and Japan studies. The very fact it exists communicates much about the uniqueness of studying Japanese film and the conditions for that research. We have endeavored to introduce institutions and resources that can help those interested in Japanese cinema explore its rich and varied world with greater depth and rigor. The first section introduces archives and libraries where you can watch films and/or consult paper or electronic resources on the cinematic heritage. The second provides a list of distributors of film prints, helping not only those of us who wish to show films on the original celluloid, but also those who want get at works unavailable on video or DVD. The third section covers bookstores, both on the net and not, that can be troves for those treasure hunters hoping to find a film book or magazine for their own or library collection. The fourth and largest portion of the book is devoted to a bibliography, not of all the books on Japanese film, but of the key works that have provided reference information for a wide range of scholars and their questions. A fifth chapter lists important online sources, and a final section tries to answer some of the questions we are frequently asked about researching Japanese film.

This guide is not intended to be exhaustive. It contains the books, journals, libraries and archives that are rich enough to reward the effort to clear the obstacles sometimes involved in their use. We are not attempting to write the English version of Tsuji Kyōhei's bibliography (74). This aims to become a *genkan* to Japanese film studies, an entryway into navigating through one of the richest cinematic archives there is. Given the unusual position Japanese film studies is in, this guide is by necessity also unusual. Just as we have, in our two decades of seriously studying Japanese film, had to personally manage the myriad of difficulties involved in that research, so this guide tries to provide a personal angle to these problems precisely so that the user can adapt it to his or her needs on the ground, so to speak. We thus provide a number of tales of trials and tribulations that hopefully can be a lesson to the reader as well. This personal perspective again means that we have not covered everything like omniscient arbiters of the discipline. Some may wonder why we picked one book and not another or why their favorite archive is relegated to "The Rest," but the quest to provide a clearer picture of the field had to start from where we stood, and we hope, with the cooperation of other scholars and users of this guide, that the conception of the field will grow in detail in the future. What we have inserted is what we have found from experience to be important. The range of publications we include in the bibliography as reference books is by necessity broad. Given the relative lack of traditional reference books such as dictionaries and encyclopedias in Japanese cinema studies, scholars must rely on a wider range of materials. Technically, almost anything can be of use, but we focus on works that a wide-range of users can reference for a variety of research purposes to obtain basic authoritative information. We take responsibility for what we include or cut, and apologize to colleagues whose work did not make that cut. The emphasis throughout is on film studies. Television will have to wait for an updated edition, if there is interest.

With each section, we offer comments both on the section as a whole as well as on important individual entries. Within many sections, we have given priority to letting users know what is most likely to help them the most, and thus have broadly ranked entries into "The Best" and "The Rest." Within those, entries are in alphabetical order, unless strong similarities (such as different editions of the same history) necessitated keeping them together, or a chronological order seemed to make better sense. Since some may still find that difficult to navigate, we have provided a basic index at the end of the book.

For archives, libraries, distributors and bookstores, we have endeavored to provide the most up-to-date contact information, including phone numbers and email addresses. We have listed the numbers you dial from inside that country (without country codes) and English websites when available (which is not very often with Japanese institutions). It is inevitable that some of this information will change over time, but we hope we have offered enough data for you to search out places even if they have moved or altered their names.

Throughout we have used modified Hepburn romanization and, with the bibliographic entries, tried to apply Library of Congress romanization rules for issues such as word division and rendering numbers. In many cases, we have consulted with the bibliographic records of major libraries like Yale and Michigan to ensure accuracy, conformity and consistency. The entries may not match those a professional bibliographer might create (for instance, we have converted all dating by imperial reign to the Western system), but these are all records that can be used to search in major library databases. We are both quite indebted to the help of librarians at our and other institutions, and we hope, as one expression of thanks, that this work can help librarians and bibliographers throughout the world single out the works that may be necessary to improve their research collections. While our bibliography is not the canon for Japanese film studies, it is a place to start exploring.

Just as we have obtained the help of many librarians, we have enjoyed the advice and suggestions of many of our colleagues and students who have commented on early versions of this work. We feel that we are all part of the effort to shape the field where we work and play. Just as this guide is, in terms of authorship, a collaborative project, we believe that the shape of the future will depend on our communal effort.

I. Collections

The Best

The following archives and libraries constitute the core resources for studying Japanese film, no matter where they are located. We do not list some of the best foreign collections of Japanese film books—which are probably the University of Michigan, Yale University, the University of Toronto, and the University of Iowa—because their collections can generally be searched online and ordered from afar through interlibrary loan.

C.V. Starr East Asian Library (Columbia University)

C.V. Starr East Asian Library
300 Kent Hall, mailcode 3901
Columbia University
1140 Amsterdam Ave.
New York, NY 10027 U.S.A.
Phone: 212-854-4318
Fax: 212-662-6286
email: starr@libraries.cul.columbia.edu
Website: www.columbia.edu/cu/lweb/indiv/eastasian/

Japanese film scholars can only look at the situation of Americanists and cry. While the scholars of Hollywood mourn the loss of so much studio history that ended up in so many dumpsters, we struggle through our bitter envy to sympathize. Japanese studios have shown no interest in sharing their internal records with historians (see the entry for the Ōtani Library below). This makes the Makino Collection at Columbia University all the more precious. Makino Mamoru is a rare species of collector; while most collectors focus fetishistically on images (posters, stills, film prints), Makino noted that the print culture of film was quickly disappearing. He amassed a precious collection that now resides at Columbia University.

The container that arrived on American shores in 2007 contained 14,576 books, 10,028 magazine and journal issues, 291 videos, 42 posters, 8 records, and 1,805 files containing tens of thousands theater programs, pamphlets, government documents, studio records and the personal papers of famous filmmakers and critics. This instantly made Columbia, along with Waseda University, the most important library for conducting Japanese film research.

One can get a glimpse at the riches studios have thrown or locked away by looking at the Tōhō materials at Columbia. Makino assembled a small, but breathtaking pot of documents from PCL and Tōhō roughly ranging from 1932 to the end of the Occupation. This includes things like the studio's own audience research, internal memoranda, regulations, correspondence, film and division budgets, and much, much more. Makino published a fine-grained, analytical index of the Tōhō materials through the Kawasaki City Museum: "Tōhō eiga bunken shiryō mokuroku (Senzen-hen) to kadai," *Kawasaki-shi Shimin Myūjiamu kiyō* 8 (1995): 79-124; "Tōhō eiga bunken shiryō mokuroku (Sengo, GHQ Senryōki-hen) to kadai," *Kawasaki-shi Shimin Myūjiamu kiyō* 9 (1996): 1-41. This provides a mouth-watering glimpse at the depth of the collection. The Columbia Library also has like documents for other periods and other studios.

Aside from his own impressive scholarship (especially on censorship, left-wing film movements, and what we call *bunkenshi* below), another quality that set Makino apart was his interest in using his collection to affect the course of Japanese film studies, an infectious spirit that has inspired the writing of the book in hand. Makino drew on his deep *oshiire* (storerooms) for many sets of influential reprint series, many of which we mention in this book. This enabled libraries the world over to acquire the core books and periodicals needed for serious Japanese film study of the prewar and wartime eras. He also opened his collection to visiting scholars, students, and curators, all of whom enriched Japanese film culture in myriad ways.

Makino tried, for many years, to sell his collection to Japanese instutitions; however, it was simply too enormous. His nibbles mostly involved breaking the collection into smaller, cheaper, chunks—the greatest fear of every great collector. Much to the disappointment of scholars and archivists everywhere, the mass of material left Japan for New York. While it is a pity this rich collection could not stay in Japan, it will at least be thoroughly catalogued and completely open to visitors. Another consolation worth noting is that many items in the collection can already be found in the Japanese libraries and archives listed below. Many of those at Columbia, once cataloged, will fall within easy reach through interlibrary loan. We, and most particularly Makino himself, look forward to seeing how it affects Japanese film studies in North America and elsewhere.

Fukuoka City Public Library Film Archive
福岡市総合図書館

Fukuoka City Public Library Film Archive
Fukuoka-shi Sōgō Toshokan

7-1 Momochihama, 3-chōme
Sawara-ku, Fukuoka 814-0001 Japan
Phone: 092-852-0600
Website: toshokan.city.fukuoka.lg.jp/docs/eizo/eizo.html

Established in 1996 and an affiliate member of FIAF (the International Federation of Film Archives) since 2004, the Fukuoka City Public Library Film Archive collects Japanese and other Asian films in addition to its primary collection of local and regional visual material, such as independent films made in Fukuoka by directors such as Ishii Sōgō. It is recognized as one of the major film archives in Japan. Fukuoka is also home to two Asian film festivals, one independent and one run by the city government (and closely affiliated with Satō Tadao). The latter has been retaining prints of the films they show, using the Film Archive as a repository. This strong emphasis on Asia makes Fukuoka City Public Library Film Archive unique among the world's film archives.

The Film Archive, in addition to preserving its 800+ film collection in a three stage film vault and exhibiting its collection at its Movie Hall Ciné-là, also operates a variety of other facilities and services. This is all outlined on their website, which also has an index to their film collection.

Gordon W. Prange Collection (University of Maryland)

Gordon W. Prange Collection
4200 Hornbake Library
University of Maryland
College Park, MD 20742 U.S.A.
Phone: 301-405-9348
Fax: 301-314-2447
email: prangebunko@umd.edu
Website: www.lib.umd.edu/prange/index.jsp

This is an extraordinary and underused collection of Occupation era publications. These are the materials that underwent censorship in MacArthur's Civil Censorship Detachment. A professor of history at the University of Maryland (and later the author of *Tora! Tora! Tora!*), Prange recognized the historical importance of the publications the detachment held, and when censorship of the Japanese media officially ended in 1949 he arranged to have everything shipped to his home institution, the University of Maryland. His collection includes virtually everything published in Japan between 1945 and 1949. This comes to 18,047 newspaper titles, 71,000 books and pamphlets, 13,799 magazines, 10,000 news agency photographs, 90 posters, and 640 maps. They also possess the personal collections of several of the censors, as well as internal government documents from the Occupation.

It should be immediately evident that this is an incredible resource for film studies, whether it's investigating local film culture through newspapers or finding photographs of film personalities. By our count, there are more than 150 film periodicals in the Prange; by way of contrast, Waseda has only 169 film journals for the entire history of cinema! To this one must add all of their books, newspapers, industry rags, pamphlets and advertisements.

There are armies of bibliographers cataloging and microfilming this massive collection. So far the magazines and newspapers are completely catalogued and indexed. They are currently working on books by subject matter.

They are also digitizing: one can get a flavor of the riches ahead by browsing their children's book collection on the website. In the meantime, they have microfilmed the newspapers and magazines. Copies are available on-site, as well as at the National Diet Library, the University of Michigan, Harvard University, and Yale University. The microfilms and fiches include censorship documents, which often attach translations and comments by the censors. Note that the Prange Collection, Harvard and Michigan all have library grants to facilitate visits to their collections by outside scholars.

There are a number of books one can turn to before plunging into the fiches, and many Asia libraries hold these indexes. They include: *Guide to the Gordon W. Prange Magazine Collection* (New York: Norman Ross Pub., 2001); Okuizumi Eizaburō, ed, *Maikurofirumu-ban senryōgun ken'etsu zasshi mokuroku, kaidai: Shōwa 20-nen - Shōwa 24-nen* (Tokyo: Yūshōdō Shoten, 1982); Noda Akemi and Sakaguchi Eiko, eds., *Merīrando Daigaku Toshokan shozō Gōdon W. Purange Bunko kyōiku tosho mokuroku: Senryōki ken'etsu kyōiku kankei tosho 1945-1949* (Tokyo: Bunsei Shoin, 2007); and Tani Eiko, ed., *Senryōka no jidōsho ken'etsu. Shiryō hen. Purange Bunko, jidō yomimono ni saguru* (Tokyo: Shin Dokushosha, 2004). The first book is the most important, as it indexes the fiche and microfilm numbers for magazines and newspapers. Film publications are not singled out, but it's fairly easy to find them in the mix.

These are certainly useful, but the most crucial resource for the first stage of research in the Prange Collection is the NDL online database (prangedb.kicx.jp). After a free and painless registration process, you can search the magazines and newspapers in breathtaking detail. Interested in what Hara Setsuko was up to during the Occupation? A search for her name comes up with 605 articles, magazine covers, and advertisements from all manner of publications. A given entry lists title, date, publication, volume/number, page number, and even if there are relevant censorship documents. The entry also provides the precise fiche or microfilm roll you need.

We can't stress how extraordinary this is, so consider one more example. Say you wanted to track down Kamei Fumio's writings during the Occupation. At other libraries and databases, one would slowly but surely find his contributions to major magazines like *Kinema junpō* and *Eiga hyōron*, usually by spending precious time at a Japanese library flipping through tables of contents. However, a few minutes on the Prange database, and you'll find those and many other riches: for example, Kamei's take on *Nihon no higeki* for *Minshū no hata,* his participation on a roundtable on women's films for the JCP magazine *Hataraku fujin,* a roundtable on cinematic eros with Miyajima Yoshio for a minor magazine in Matsuyama, an article entitled "Uso bakari no eiga" for *Shikoku bunshū,* or his views on war responsibility of filmmakers in an obscure May 1946 newsletter.

Pick any topic. There are amazing things in Prange and they are remarkably easy to find. What's more, the library will make copies for a nominal fee, and presumably one of the universities listed above will accommodate ILL requests.

Image Forum
イメージフォーラム

Image Forum
2-10-2 Shibuya
Shibuya-ku, Tokyo 150-0002 Japan
Phone: 03-5766-0116
email : info@imageforum.co.jp
Website: www.imageforum.co.jp

Arguably the main institution dealing with experimental film in Japan, Image Forum can be traced back to the late 1960s and the Japan Underground Center. While maintaining strong ties with Terayama Shūji, it was the experimental filmmaker Kawanaka Nobuhiro and his wife Tomiyama Katsue who have formed the pillars of this organization over the years. It took the name Image Forum in 1977 and functioned not only as a cinémathèque but also as a publisher and a small film school that has generated such filmmakers as Mochizuki Rokurō and Ōki Hiroyuki. Its annual festival, held in Tokyo with versions presented in Fukuoka, Osaka and Yokohama, is the centerpiece of experimental film and video in Japan. Long in Yotsuya, Image Forum moved to Shibuya in 1999 to establish its own commercial theater. It is thus not a research institution, although the festival and the cinémathèque are still important opportunities to catch rare experimental work. As a distributor, however, it is an essential institution to contact if you want to view or screen experimental works. Still, one must remember that it does not represent all of Japanese experimental film. There are "non-" or "anti-" Image Forum groups and their activities should be taken into account as well.

Kawakita Memorial Film Institute
川喜多記念映画文化財団

Kawakita Kinen Eiga Bunka Zaidan

Kawakita Memorial Building
18 Ichiban-chō
Chiyoda-ku, Tokyo 102-0082 Japan
Phone: 03-3265-3281
Fax: 03-3265-3276
email: kmfi@kawakita-film.or.jp
Website: www.kawakita-film.or.jp

The Kawakita Memorial Film Institute was originally formed as the Japan Film Library Council in 1960 by Kawakita Kashiko and her husband Kawakita Nagamasa, the president of the film distributor Tōwa Eiga. The two had been central in introducing both foreign art cinema in Japan and Japanese films abroad, and for many years the Film Institute was the primary source of help to foreign scholars, showing them subtitled films from their collection and helping with stills and other resources. It still tries to do that, but in an age where the major studios are insisting on their rights in every area, the Kawakita Institute's usefulness has decreased. It still contains a significant collection of film magazines (especially some prewar ones that are not readily available elsewhere), press sheets (nearly 15,000), pamphlets (nearly 7,000), and international film festival catalogs (one rather unique feature). They also have a very large collection of film prints. Much of these materials can now be searched online and some of the collection is immediately available on open stacks.

There is a now-defunct index of their films published in the early 1980s: *Zaidan Hōjin Kawakita Kinen Eiga Bunka Zaidan zōsho mokuroku: Washo no bu* (Tokyo: Kawakita Kinen Eiga Bunka Zaidan, 1982). The book collection is not that unique, but they also have materials on Ozu (see www.um.u-tokyo.ac.jp/japanese/publish_db/1999ozu/japanese/14.html for a sample), and donated collections, such as those from the film critics Yodogawa Nagaharu and Noguchi Hisamitsu. Perhaps their best archival materials pertain to films the Kawakitas themselves distributed. By all means ask what they have and you may be pleasantly surprised.

Some of the Kawakitas' collection is still being processed. But they will no longer readily supply stills for Japanese films unless you have permission from the company (which now usually requires payment), or the film is so old copyright has long expired. Stills cost ¥700. They are also less capable of screening films for researchers, though if you have a letter from your university they can still occasionally do it (for no fee). Much of their materials are on site, but it is advisable to contact them beforehand to see what is currently off site (their files from films the Kawakitas distributed are in storage and require advance notice). They very well may have some amazing finds, but with photocopying costing ¥100 (¥60 for students), the Kawakita Institute is usually the place to visit if you can't find what you want somewhere else. Do note they are only open 1-5 on weekdays.

Kawasaki City Museum
川崎市市民ミュージアム

Kawasaki-shi Shimin Myūjiamu
1-2 Todoroki
Nakahara-ku, Kawasaki, Kanagawa 211-0052 Japan
Phone: 044-754-4500
Fax: 044-754-4533
email: art@kawasaki-museum.jp
Website: www.kawasaki-museum.jp

The Kawasaki City Museum was founded in 1988 as one of many museums built around the country to showcase local art, history and culture—the *"furusato"* or hometown—but while the Museum has always fulfilled its role of researching and preserving Kawasaki's archeological treasures, it has done more than many local museums to create collections nation-wide in scope, especially in the often-neglected popular arts like film, manga, and video. The cinémathèque, while mostly showing films on weekends, is a major venue for film retrospectives (and almost as cheap as the Film Center), and the museum itself often hosts fascinating exhibitions centered on popular culture topics. While somewhat inconveniently located, it is one of the primary film sites in the Kantō area that is definitely worth the trek. Aaron spent practically every weekend of his first summer in Japan at the Kawasaki City Museum, so it is one of his film *furusato*.

Having had a number of important film historians, such as Makino Mamoru and Okumura Masaru, serve as staff curators, the Kawasaki City Museum has built up a significant research collection that is especially strong in documentary and video art. Until recently, with a large viewing room where anyone could view old and new films without a reservation, the Museum was one of the best places to see movies on video if you did not have access to Tsutaya or a university library. That facility has been greatly reduced, but researchers and residents can still see many works on video, sometimes without a reservation. Their strongest collections relate to documentary (the wartime *Nihon nyūsu* newsreel, the *Kanagawa nyūsu* newsreel, the Ushiyama Jun'ichi Collection of television documentaries, GHQ Occupation-era films, etc.), video art (the Scan Collection, featuring works shown at Japan's first video art gallery), and television commercials (which are still being actively collected). Many commercially produced DVDs and videos can also be viewed. The Museum has over 300 films on 35mm, focusing on independent production companies like ATG, the Kindai Eiga Kyōkai, Gekidan Mingei, and Argo Pictures, but it has no facilities for researchers to view these works (you have to wait for them to show it at the cinémathèque, or get permission from the copyright holder to rent out the print to screen it yourself). Their collection of over 2,500 16mm prints is more accessible, however, since they can let you view them on a Steenbeck. Again the focus is on documentary, with many works by Kamei Fumio, Prokino, Ogawa Shinsuke, Tsuchimoto Noriaki, and Matsumoto Toshio, as well as on educational films and animation. (It is now out-of-date, but they did publish a list of the 168 films in their collection as of 1988: *Shuzō eiga tōroku* [Kawasaki City: Kawasaki-shi Shimin Myūjiamu, 1989]). One must apply beforehand to see such works (contact the film or video curator by e-mail or fax first), but there is no fee. The museum also has many foreign films, but only their Japanese film prints can be searched in their online database.

Apart from films, their collection of movie-related printed matter is definitely not as strong as other Kantō institutions (they are better in manga or related fields), with about 2,500 books mostly focused on criticism and movie stars, divided between open and closed stacks. In terms of special collections, they have many wartime and postwar theater pamphlets (a database can be searched on-site), about 500 postwar posters, and a considerable amount of production-related documents for PR film companies like Nyūsu Eigasha. Personal collections include those of the art directors Kubo Kazuo and Kimura Takeo, the screenwriter Ide Masato, and the director Kumashiro Tatsumi.

Kōbe Planet Film Archive
神戸プラネット映画資料図書館

Planet Bibliotheque de Cinema/Puranetto Eiga Shiryō Toshokan
206 Shirono Bldg
4-41 Banzai-chō
Kita-ku, Osaka 530-0027 Japan
Phone: 06-6364-2165
Fax: 06-6312-8232
email: planet1@m11.alpha-net.ne.jp
Website: www.alpha-net.ne.jp/users2/planet1/

Kōbe Planet Film Archive/Kōbe Eiga Shiryōkan
Asuta Kunizuka Ichibankan Hokutō 2F 201
5-5-1 Udezuka-chō, Nagata-ku
Kōbe 653-0036 Japan
Phone/Fax: 078-754-8039
email: info@kobe-eiga.net
Website: www.kobe-eiga.net
Copies: Self-serve at the 7-11 around the corner

Planet is a fixture of the Kansai film scene, and one of the best resources for film study in the region. It is unquestionably the most unusual film archive in Japan. Formed in 1974 as a film library, it has steadily grown under the leadership of Yasui Yoshio. In 1995 they added a mini-theater as part of an independent screening movement, running an eclectic schedule of screenings throughout the year. They have over 5,000 films in all formats, 10,000 books and journals, 10,000 posters, and much, much more. Planet amassed this collection in a rather unconventional manner. As one of the key centers of Kansai film culture, many filmmakers and fans have donated their personal collections over the years. When distributors or theaters have gone out of business, they either sell their equipment and records to Yasui or donate them outright. Their theaters are cobbled together with equipment torn out of bankrupt theaters.

In 2007 they moved the bulk of the collection to the new Kōbe Planet Film Archive, leaving only some core reference materials and journals in Osaka. The new archive has a 23-seat theater and a reading room.

Planet is both the easiest and most difficult collection to use in Japan. Yasui is generally amenable to helping any researcher in need. In contrast to the excessive restrictions of the Film Center, he will sometimes show researchers films on flatbeds and actually allows them to make copies of magazines by taking materials to a neighborhood copyshop. It is the most informal and friendly institution in the country.

Unfortunately, there is a downside. The move to Kōbe allowed them to consolidate several storage facilities worth of paper and film. However, their cataloging system amounts to three categories: the room full of films, the room full of equipment, and the room full of paper. Each of these is a *katatsumuri*-like space—a maze of rows just wide enough to squeeze through. That is to say, there is a problem with access: items exist to the extent that Yasui remembers he has them, and they are accessible only if he can find them. Nothing has been catalogued and it may remain in its current, elegantly simple, trifurcated structure.

It is definitely worth contacting them with specific questions, and they can answer them to the best of their ability. They have many unique materials, particularly regarding Kansai film production, distribution and exhibition. Yasui is also a fount of knowledge regarding the Kansai film world, as well as the general areas of animation and documentary. For all these reasons Planet is precious, but it is also hit and miss.

Library of Congress (LOC)

Motion Picture and Television Reading Room
101 Independence Ave. SE
James Madison Building, LM 336
Washington, D.C. 20540-4690 U.S.A.
Phone: 202-707-8572
Fax: 202-707-2371
email: via webform on homepage

Website: www.loc.gov/rr/mopic/

The core Japanese film collection is in the Captured Foreign Films Collection, and has approximately 200 feature films, 700 educational films and an unspecified number of Japanese newsreels. This makes it significantly larger than the comparable captured records group at the National Archives. It is technically the most convenient location for viewing prewar Japanese cinema on film in North America since there are many rare works here, it is free, and you can watch them on a Steenbeck. There are problems, however. Beyond the fact that viewing of films in general is restricted to researchers and that you have to make appointments well in advance, the Japanese collection is not well cataloged. It is not accessible online and the card catalog available at the Reading Room contains mistakes (although Aaron once sent them a lot of corrections!). How do you then know what they have? One way is just to look at what prewar films are referenced by early scholars of Japanese film like Noël Burch and David Bordwell. Many they viewed at the Library of Congress; even if they watched some in Japan, the core of the National Film Center's prewar collection in the 1970s and early 1980s were these captured films that were returned in the late 1960s.

Easier to find are their postwar films on film or video, most of which were submitted through copyright deposit. There are no statistics for the size of these holdings, but they are significant. The catalog lists more than 500 film prints and videos in the Japanese language, but the library says there are surely more. Some can be searched through Moving Image Collections (mic.imtc.gatech.edu).

The Library of Congress also has a major Japanese film book collection, not to mention many collections of prewar Japanese government documents from a number of ministries.

Matsuda Film Productions
マツダ映画社

Matsuda Eigasha
3-18-4 Tōwa
Adachi-ku, Tokyo 120-0003 Japan
Phone: 03-3605-9981
Fax: 03-3605-9982
email: katuben@attglobal.net
Website: www.matsudafilm.com
Copies: generally not allowed

In the postwar era, Matsuda Film Productions has played a vital role in the preservation and performance of silent film culture. Matsuda Shunsui established the company in 1952 around a collection of films and memorabilia. A fan of silent film and the *benshi,* Matsuda studied to become a *benshi* himself. Using his collection as a core, he created the Friends of Silent Films Association in 1959 to document silent film history and stage regular screenings of silent films with live *benshi* and musical accompaniment (upcoming performances are listed on their website). They have also published *benshi*-narrated videos, a DVD-ROM database (157), and the long-running *Kurashikku eiga nyūsu* (94). In recent years they have increasingly internationalized their activities through the help of Urban Connections, a very welcome development. After Matsuda Shunsui's passing, his sons have carried on the business—and the tradition.

The Matsuda collection is considerable. It includes approximately 500 books, 500 journals and magazines, 100 scenarios, silent era projectors, *kamishibai* card sets and paraphernalia, and some 10,000 other items like posters, still photographs, programs and the like. There is no real inventory or catalog of this material, so something "exists" to the extent that staff members have seen and remembered it. They suspect the staff has a solid grasp of 60% of the collection, with as much as 10% that has never really been handled.

The film collection is the main feature here. If we include fragments and partial prints, they have around 1,000 titles. The most important of these are listed on their webpage. The quality of these prints is variable, as they generally made safety film copies without cleaning and restoration. Matsuda holds about 2,000 videos as well. The DVDs and tapes they have produced for sale all have *benshi* narration, and they are gradually adding subtitles; these may be purchased through their website.

Finally, it must be pointed out that Matsuda Film Productions is a private company. They are perfectly happy to show researchers films, videos, and the more unique materials they hold. However, this is strictly on a for-pay basis and requires reservations. Likewise, copies of stills for publication may be readily purchased. If you visit, it is best to make an appointment.

One other special feature is their rental system. Matsuda maintains a team of skilled *benshi* and musicians (most notably *benshi* Sawato Midori and pianist Yanashita Mie) to compliment their film and equipment collection. They are happy to arrange screenings anywhere in the world.

Museum of Kyoto Film Library Centre
京都府京都文化博物館

Museum of Kyoto Film Library Centre
Kyōto-fu Kyōto Bunka Hakubutsukan
Sanjō Takakura, 623-1 Higashi Kata-machi
Nakagyo-ku, Kyoto-shi, Kyoto-fu 604-8183 Japan
Phone: 075-222-0888
Fax: 075-222-0889

email: office@bunpaku.or.jp
Website: www.bunpaku.or.jp

The friendly Museum of Kyoto Film Library Centre, otherwise known as the "Bunpaku," began its fine collection of books, journals, and films in 1971 and established its Film Library in 1988. For many years it was dominated by one collection: the very large and wonderful personal library of director Itō Daisuke. According to film scholar Itakura Fumiaki, who catalogued the material, this alone is constituted by 7,489 books, 10,000 magazine issues, and 50 boxes of treasure. The latter includes Itō's memos, various scenario drafts (including those he used during shooting), and still photographs.

In the intervening years, more and more Kyoto filmmakers have donated materials. Major collections include critic Ogi Masahiro, director Mori Kazuo, screenwriter Kessoku Shinji, collector Okuda Kazuto, sound recordist Kurashima Tōru, screenwriter Susukita Rokuhei, and Yamanaka Sadao. The collection holds some objects that take the breath away, such as Makino Shōzō's death mask or the English-Japanese dictionary Yamanaka Sadao used as a student which he turned into a flip book by drawing *chanbara* scenes in the margins.

The Bunpaku also has a climate conditioned film vault with nearly 800 films and a large collection of raw audio tapes from Daiei productions. These may be impossible to access, simply for lack of resources. However, the museum has also been collecting videos, CD-ROMs and DVDs, which can be freely viewed on site. For more information on the Bunpaku see Moriwaki Kiyotaka, "Kyoto-fū Kyoto Bunka Hakubutsukan (Eizōbumon)," *NFC* 25 (May-June 1999): 13-15, as well as the handsome exhibition catalog they once published: *Kyōto eizō fesuta: Yume to roman de tsuzuru firumu runessansu* (Kyoto: Kyoto Bunka Hakubutsukan, 2003).

National Archives and Records Administration (NARA)

Motion Picture, Sound, and Video Research Room
National Archives at College Park
8601 Adelphi Road
College Park, MD 20740-6001 U.S.A.
Phone: 301-837-0526
email: mopix@nara.gov
Website: www.archives.gov/research/formats/visit-motion-picture-room.html

The National Archives and Records Administration is the archive for the United States government. In principle, the records produced by the U.S. government are public domain; they can be classified, but otherwise they are preserved and freely available to anyone. One can even dub a film off a flatbed using a video camera. Because any document—paper, still photograph or film—is the property of the people, bureacrats have no say in their fate; only archivists can choose not to preserve things.

Why would the U.S. National Archive be a great place to study Japanese cinema? First, because the United States carefully studied its enemies during the Second World War. But also because Japan was essentially American territory between 1945 and 1952 (1972 for Okinawa), and because between 1945 and 1949 Americans were busy censoring every film and film publication. The records left over from all that work are preserved in their Maryland archive (in addition to the nearby Prange Collection).

There were two offices responsible for managing the Japanese film industry during the Occupation, one civil and the other military. Here are their record numbers, which will make navigation on the bewildering online ARC catalog a bit easier: Civil Information and Education Section (ARC Identifier: 61850, Local Identifier: 331) and the Civil Censorship Detachment (ARC Identifier: 486860).

To get a sense for what is in this collection—which includes everything from reports to memoranda to scenarios—read Kyoko Hirano's *Mr. Smith Goes to Tokyo: The Japanese Cinema under the American Occupation, 1945-1952* (Washington: Smithsonian Institution Press, 1992). This is an excellent history of the Occupation era. However, considering the fact that this is the period of Japanese cinema with the richest archive, Hirano's book is nothing other than the foundation for much future work.

NARA also has a few important Japanese films, notably the co-produced *The Effects of the Atomic Bomb on Hiroshima and Nagasaki* (1946). Also, as the American troops swept towards Japan during World War II, they "captured" prints in local studios and movie theaters. These prints were sent back to the U.S., where they were studied and recycled into U.S. propaganda documentaries. There are significant holdings of *Nihon nyūsu,* including versions in other Asian languages, as well as a number of famous documentaries from the 1930s and early 1940s. This makes them easier to access than in Japan, where NHK will sell you segments by the second and the National Film Center charges researchers by the half-hour for viewings (those in Japan should turn to the Kawasaki City Museum [14-15] and the Shōwa-kan [47-48]). Most of the films are in the Collection of Foreign Records Seized of the Military Intelligence Division (Local Identifier: 242 MID). There are many more films at the Library of Congress (16-17).

NARA has literally thousands of films from the Occupation era. There is an amazing collection of 16mm color film on the Occupation of the main islands between 1945 and 1952. This was mainly shot by Harry Mimura under the auspices of the Strategic Bombing Survey. Most of these films are unedited footage—a raw visual record of Japan at a crucial moment in its modern history.

The Americans also shot over 2,000 16mm films in Okinawa during the war and the subsequent Occupation; they have yet to be fully catalogued, but there is a 67-page paper index of them (the archive will share this upon request). They are scattered through 32 record groups. An excellent starting place for approaching these records is a publication by Nakamoto Kazuhiko from the Okinawa Prefectural Archive (141), which has repatriated much of this footage to Japan.

The only problem with NARA is its electronic catalog. Named ARC, it offers nothing but frustration. We have found important Japanese films on their old card catalog that didn't show up in ARC searches. Titles we know they hold can require some dedicated searching. Luckily, the archivists are on top of their holdings and extremely helpful in person or on the phone.

This is a relatively limited slice of time. The films are mostly unedited rushes and the paper materials are best suited to projects on censorship and bureaucracy. However, as one of the few pots of studio records available to researchers, NARA is of outsized importance for such a limited collection.

The National Diet Library (NDL)
国立国会図書館

Kokuritsu Kokkai Toshokan
1-10-1 Nagata-chō
Chiyoda-ku, Tokyo 100-8924 Japan
Phone: 03-3581-2331
Website: www.ndl.go.jp

The National Diet Library has a wide variety of resources for the Japanese film scholar. Working in the library sometimes feels like a slow-motion sequence. Book retrieval takes serious time, copying is an expensive hassle, and the food in the cafeteria is horrible. For this reason, many researchers choose to do their work at other venues. However, the Diet Library should not be missed. For some projects it is absolutely essential.

The core of the library would probably be the books and periodicals. Upon its establishment in 1948, it became the national depository for all publications in Japan. You can generally bet that they'll have the book you are looking for. They'll definitely have it if it is a postwar publication and not manga or pornographic. Minor periodicals, especially from the prewar period, are another matter. They do have a massive collection of newspapers from around Japan. These have an enormous amount of information about local film exhibition and film culture.

One little known corner of the library is the Ongaku-Eizō Shiryōshitsu. Recent tweaking of the Diet Library law requires that publishers of music and film also deposit their new materials. Their music collection goes back to the prewar period (15,000 78s, 100,000 EPs, 175,000 LPs and 261,000 CDs), so this would be one place to find recordings of film soundtracks. They started collecting moving image materials much later—and they estimate they are actually receiving only 60% of what is put into distribution—but their collection is already impressive. As of 2008, they hold 66,000 items on LD, DVD, and VHS. The Ongaku-Eizō Shiryōshitsu has a row of booths where these may be viewed. Unfortunately, their cataloging format is ill-conceived, so it is difficult to search by director, staff, actor or studio. The only subject words that are linked are video series. Be prepared to search primarily by release title. This room is also where some of the basic reference books for film are located, although the pickings are slim.

Another important room is the Kensei Shiryōshitsu, which preserves government records. Their most important holdings are complete microfilm copies of the U.S. National Archives (19-21) materials from the Occupation (GHQ/SCAP, USSBS, USCAR; for more information see www.ndl.go.jp/jp/data/kensei_shiryo/senryo/CIE.html). In one crucial respect, the Diet Library is a better place to conduct research on the Occupation than the U.S. National Archives itself. While the National Archives has catalogued down to the record group and box level, the Diet Library has actually indexed everything in the boxes. A search on their database produces their holdings in impressive detail. Unfortunately, the only place one can access this computerized catalog is in the Kensei Shiryōshitsu, but there are plans to put it on the internet sometime in the future. This is also the room you'll find the microformed newspapers and magazines from the Prange Collection (10-12).

The NDL website has a research guide for film related statistics: www.ndl.go.jp/jp/data/theme/theme_honbun_101107.html. This contains some resources not included in this book, so it is worth a look.

Like the other government document repositories in Japan, the Diet Library has initiated some interesting digitizing projects. The most significant is their entire collection of Meiji era books, which includes some of the first publications about cinema.

The NDL also has a major branch in the Kansai area called the Kansaikan located in the middle of nowhere between Kyoto and Osaka. Since it duplicates many of the paper materials in the Tokyo Library, either on paper or on microfilm, it can be of use to those living in the Kansai area. The Kansaikan, however, has many scientific and Asia-related materials not in Tokyo, and there are certain government records, such as the reports on Monkashō-funded research since 1983, that only it collects.

This branch is also the only place one can view all of the nation's Ph.D. dissertations. As more and more scholars actually finish their degrees, and as the discipline begins to demand more primary research, this is a growing resource. There is a dedicated online database for dissertations on their homepage.

Finally, the Diet Library does have a copying service, for a fee, for scholars living anywhere in the world. This does require registering first in person.

National Film Center (NFC)
東京国立近代美術館フィルムセンター

Tokyo Kokuritsu Kindai Bijutsukan Film Center
3-7-6 Kyōbashi
Chūō-ku, Tokyo 104-0031 Japan
Phone: 03-5777-8600
Fax: 03-3561-0830
Website: www.momat.go.jp/FC/fc.html
Copies: 30 yen/page for B&W; 100 yen/page for color
Digital cameras are prohibited

This is the primary film archive in Japan. Because it is a national institution, it holds the largest collection of Japanese films in the world. For a long time, however, as a government organ, it was hampered by bureaucratic red tape and a lack of funding, a situation that made it very hard to use—especially if one wanted to see films for research. Matters have considerably improved since the National Film Center became an "independent administrative agency" (*dokuritsu gyōsei hōjin*); it is now the "usable" NFC, although one still does need to learn how to jump through the various hoops to get what one wants.

Despite getting a late start, having been founded only in 1952, they have 25,000 books, 30,000 scripts, 57,500 posters, 490,000 still photographs, and a large collection of cameras and projectors. Their prewar film stills, obtained from the offices of *Kinema junpō*, are unparalleled. The curators have culled all this for a wonderful permanent exhibit, "Japanese Film Heritage," where a number of important early films are running on a loop. They also have thematic exhibits, often in conjunction with screenings.

The marvelous collection of Misono Kyōhei has become the core for their holdings of posters, stills, and theater programs, but compared to other institutions, the NFC holds a relatively small number of personal libraries of film-related people. Beyond those of Atsugi Taka, Kosugi Isamu, Motoki Sōjirō, and Fujita Toshiya, probably the most important collection of personal papers is that of Kinugasa Teinosuke. This is a major collection of 50,000 items that arrived in 41 boxes. Nakatani Masanao, who helped first collate the collection, has described it in *Nokoreshi mono: Taishō-ki no Kinugasa Teinosuke shiryō* (Tokyo: NHK Hōsō Bunka Kenkyūjo, 1997). The NFC also does not have many internal studio documents. They are continually processing other donations, so it is worth asking a curator about what is new, as they may very well have some hidden jewels.

Because of their recent establishment, the archive has poured most of its energies into saving what little is left of Japanese cinema on unstable nitrate. This also means they have neglected their paper materials in comparison, so their collection of journals is mainly useful to fill in the holes at Waseda or the Ōtani Library. The strength of their library is primarily in monographs, and they have recently been compiling a bibliographic catalog, available online, which indexes some materials other bibliographic indexes do not.

The main attraction of the National Film Center is the film archive. It preserves over 50,000 titles, of which nearly 47,000 are Japanese. Breaking the Japanese films down, there are nearly 8,000 fiction features, over 17,000 *bunka eiga,* 1,800 animated films, over 11,000 newsreels, and almost 4,500 television movies and programs. It collects in every era, genre and mode of cinema. The controlled storage is in Sagamihara, a couple hours from central Tokyo. Prints are shipped in to Kyōbashi for screenings and study. They have two public screening rooms that feature thematic seasons of films—the cheapest film screenings in Japan. There is also a smaller screening room for private viewing.

Seeing films for research purposes is not easy, but it is doable. Almost all of their fiction films are searchable on their online database, so you can first check there to see what is available (although they warn that not all of those films, because of the condition of the print, may actually be viewable). If you know what films you want to see, or if you want to check if they have films from other genres like documentary, you can then contact the NFC by fax to begin the process of applying for a screening. You must allow at least two weeks for the process and specify how many people will see the films. You can have as many attend the screening as can fit in any one of their three theaters (as long as you are not charging people admission or publicizing it), but the bigger theaters are harder to book. The NFC does not allow researchers to view films on flatbeds, a serious impediment to close textual analysis and far from the norm in international archival practice. Nevertheless, about 1,000 titles from their collection have been put on video for viewing. You have to follow the same procedure and pay the same amount for a video screening as for a film, but you can view it in a separate video booth. (Do note, however, that since you are charged for every 30 minutes, rewinding and reviewing scenes adds to the cost.) For screenings, those associated with educational institutions pay ¥2,625 for every 30 minutes; others pay twice that.

You follow basically the same procedure for use of stills and posters. Since there is no online database, you should fax them to ask if they have what you are looking for. If they do, you can then schedule a time to visit to take a look. They will not send copies via e-mail. Technically, they charge money even to look at stills and posters, but this charge is usually waived if you order copies later on. They charge ¥5,250 for each still, although the cost can be halved or even waived depending on your circumstances. For posters, you have to make the photographic copy yourself, either with your own camera or by hiring a photographer; in either case, you pay the NFC ¥7,000 per poster.

For both film screenings and copies of stills and posters, in principle only groups or institutions can apply; private individuals cannot. You can still see the film or the stills alone, but you must have your university or, if you are writing a book as an independent researcher, your publisher make the application. The NFC will provide the form (in Japanese) which you then fill out and have some higher-up at your institution sign.

As with many institutions in Japan, the Film Center is very sensitive about copyright, so don't expect to easily do frame grabs from prints in their collection (though they may allow that in special cases). They also house prints under certain contractual conditions, so don't even try to ask for a VHS copy of a film for your own personal, off-site viewing.

One still wishes the NFC could do more for researchers, especially compared to foreign institutions, but for the time being we should be thankful for the strides they have made. The Film Center is notoriously under-funded and under-staffed, but unlike other institutions in Japan, the curators are all top film scholars who can offer a fount of information and advice when they have time. They are trying their very best to promote Japanese film; we can only hope that the Japanese government, the film industry, and Japanese society as a whole better promote film research by increasing funding and reducing all the obstacles.

Pacific Film Archive (PFA)

Pacific Film Archive
Berkeley Art Museum
2625 Durant Avenue #2250
Berkeley CA 94720-2250 U.S.A.
Phone: 510-642-1437
email: bampfa@berkeley.edu
Website: www.bampfa.berkeley.edu/pfalibrary
Access fee to library: $3
Digital cameras are prohibited

The Pacific Film Archive has the largest collection of Japanese films outside of Japan, and perhaps the largest in the world with reasonable access to researchers (unlike the National Film Center, they will provide a flatbed for close analysis). The core of their collection is comprised from several donations of B-movies from Daiei and Nikkatsu. This makes them particularly important to those studying popular film culture of the 1950s and 1960s. The main collection holds 10,000 films and videos, of which there are 1,500 Japanese films and trailers. What's more, most of these Japanese prints were originally shown in Japanese-American theaters so they are also subtitled in English.

A searchable database on their website lists all their films. However, more detailed information on the Daiei films is published in a thick catalog: *Films in the Collection of the Pacific Film Archive, Volume I: Daiei Motion Picture Co., Ltd. Japan (140).*

This is a friendly and open archive. Depending on the condition of prints, they are happy when researchers use their precious films. There is a ten-seat screening room for 16mm, 8mm, and video. Projectionists are provided for film. Films on 35mm can be viewed on a flatbed. Screening fees vary depending on one's connections to the museum and UC Berkeley.

There are other reasons to visit the PFA. Their collections include over 7,600 books, 150 journal titles, 7,500 posters, 35,000 stills, and 1,500 audiotapes of filmmakers who have appeared at the Pacific Film Archive. Unfortunately, only a fraction of these cover Japanese film. They do have partial runs of *Kinema junpō, Kindai eiga* and *Eiga fan* for the 1950s and 1960s—the period of strength in their film collection. They also have a boxfull of studio and distributor catalogs aimed at the English-language market (mostly from the 1960s). This is supplemented by a fair collection of Japanese-language film periodicals and books in the University's C.V. Starr East Asian Library, a ten-minute walk away from the PFA.

If you are unable to make a trip to Berkeley, the archivists will supply some reference work over the phone. If this help takes more than 20 minutes, they offer a consultation service charging fairly minimal fees.

Another special resource one can use from afar is their clipping file, which fills rows of vertical files scattered throughout the archive. There are over 95,000 files, but regrettably few for Japanese film. These are mainly restricted to canonical directors and films, and are of particular interest for their festival and retrospective catalogs. Quite a bit of this is available online through CineFiles, a database drawing on the clipping files. Anyone working on major directors should try a search. It's likely to produce some unusual items. It's an exemplary service that other archives could learn from.

Setagaya Literary Museum
世田谷文学館

Setagaya Bungakukan
1-10-10 Minami Karasuyama
Setagaya-ku, Tokyo 157-0062 Japan
Phone: 03-5374-9111
Fax: 03-5374-9120
email: webmaster@setabun.net
Website: www.setabun.or.jp

The Setagaya Literary Museum came about through a series of happy coincidences that resulted in one of the finest film collections in Japan. The

Setagaya area of Tokyo had a modern art museum, but their definition of art was basically limited to painting and sculpture. In 1995, they decided to create a literary museum to celebrate the high concentration of authors that lived in this *ku* (ward). While they were at it, they decided to stretch the definition of author to include screenwriters, recognizing the equally impressive number of filmmakers that also lived in the neighborhood thanks to the nearby PCL/Tōhō lot. The museum created a modest "corner" exhibit they dubbed the "Eiga Mecca." The mecca attracted a surprising number of film devotees, and soon local filmmakers were donating their personal collections and libraries. They were thrilled at the attention. Things snowballed and by 2000 the museum's exhibition turned into the Setagaya Film Festival, which combines screenings in a new 35mm space with special exhibitions built around their now impressive collection (ask to see the *shiryōshū* they've published for each festival and you can see a list of the wonderful archival material they've displayed). The festivals are built around filmmakers or themes: costume design, the work of Kurosawa Akira, Kobayashi Masaki, Inagaki Hiroshi, science fiction films, Japanese musicals, Mifune Toshirō, screenwriting, and Ichikawa Kon. They also bring in *benshi* and major speakers. It's an event not to be missed.

And the archive is also worth a visit. They've collected 23,109 books, 28,584 film magazines, 4,246 scripts, 2,062 posters and *chirashi*, 23,207 items like set and costume design drawings, and 5,389 manuscripts. The centerpiece of the collection is the personal library of Kobayashi Masaki (a large collection with over 2,700 items). However, they also have wonderful materials from the other filmmakers listed above, in addition to precious donations from Tōhō production staff. The museum also has an important cache of documents from the Tōhō strike, including 63 sketches of the labor actions.

Finally, don't leave the museum without a sidetrip to the museum cafe, which is guarded by Godzilla—the *real* rubber Godzilla!

Shōchiku Ōtani Library
松竹大谷図書館

Shōchiku Ōtani Toshokan
ADK Shōchiku Square 3F
1-13-1 Tsukiji
Chūō-ku, Tokyo 104-0045 Japan
Phone: 03-5550-1694
Fax: 03-5550-1642
Webpage: www.shochiku.co.jp/shochiku-otani-toshokan

The Shōchiku Ōtani Library was created in 1956 to commemorate the awarding of an Order of Culture to Ōtani Takejirō, one of the founders of Shōchiku. It is a theater and film library, covering Shōchiku's two main areas of business, with a primary focus on non-published materials, specifically scripts for stage and screen. There is an emphasis on films and plays Shōchiku has produced or distributed, but it also has materials for other studio films. While the number of prewar scripts is limited (and often treated as rare books, which means no photocopying), they estimate they have material on about 90% of Shōchiku's postwar productions, which can include several generations of the script, pressbooks, theater programs, stills, and posters. They also have a major collection of books and magazines, for a grand total of about 350,000 items, but unfortunately only a limited number of internal studio documents (they mainly have things like company newsletters and publicity scrapbooks). Like other Japanese archives these days, the Ōtani is very sensitive about copyright, so since they do the copying for you (for orders of more than 10 pages [at ¥50 per page], you have to pick it up the next business day or pay to have it mailed), it is hard to copy entire scripts. Generally speaking, they do not supply stills for publication. They have started to digitize their catalog for in-house use, but most records are still on cards; however, their subject catalog, using their own peculiar system, is somewhat useful. Stacks are completely closed. They are mainly open 10-5 on weekdays (with lunchtime off), but since it is often closed on special occasions, especially during August, it is best to check the homepage before visiting.

Tsubouchi Memorial Theatre Museum (Waseda University)
早稲田大学坪内博士記念演劇博物館

Tsubouchi Hakase Kinen Engeki Hakubutsukan
Waseda University
1-6-1 Nishi-Waseda
Shinjuku-ku, Tokyo 169-8050 Japan
Phone: 03-5286-1829
Fax: 03-5273-4398
Webpage: www.waseda.jp/enpaku/index-e.html
Digital copies are possible with a fee.

Waseda makes serious research into Japanese cinema a matter of pure pleasure. We love this place. The Tsubouchi Memorial Theatre Museum, housed in a pretty 1928 reproduction of a 16th century English theater, is such a fantastic, deep and open collection that it virtually offers one-stop shopping. This is the library we visit on every trip to Japan. The larger collection includes all the other performing arts, but their film collection is probably the largest in Japan with 6,700 books, 169 journals, and 25,000 scripts—and yet more materials await cataloging. There is an *utsushie* (lantern slide) collection, posters, stills, programs, catalogs and the like. A hundred Japanese videos are available on-site (they also have prints, but those are not publicly available). Their library online catalog, WINE, is an indispensable database for information on Japanese film publications.

Another important resource they have is a strong collection of theater newsletters (*eigakan kanhō* or *eigakan shūhō*). There are 272 titles from theaters all over Japan. The collection covers the years 1926 to 1943. These can be a rich resource for research on prewar/wartime film culture, providing hints about the conditions of the local reception context. Many contain original writing or interviews. Thanks to *The Complete Dictionary of Japanese Movies* (94-95), they are remarkably easy to use. *The Complete Dictionary of Japanese Movies* gives both release dates and the theater(s) every film premiered at. Using this information, you can zero in on the relevant programs in the collection. (Many other libraries, especially Kawasaki (14-15), Columbia (8-9), and the National Film Center, have collections of these prewar theater programs.)

In addition to these published works, the library has slowly acquired a few personal collections. These include the libraries of Inagaki Hiroshi, Yamatoya Atsushi, *benshi* Komada Kōyō, Wakayama Genzō, and Sugimura Haruko.

The reference room is comfortable, contains all the standard reference books and the complete runs of *Kinema junpō*, *Nihon eiga*, and *Kokusai eiga shinbun*, and you are bound to meet a friend or two there because everyone knows Waseda is by far the best place to research Japanese cinema. Photocopying is the cheapest of the major archives and they let you do it yourself with regular items. The museum itself is always worth a visit; the temporary exhibits often include film-related themes.

The Rest

Anthology Film Archives

Anthology Film Archives
32 Second Avenue
New York, NY 10003 U.S.A.
Telephone: 212-505-5181
Fax: 212-477-2714
email: robert@anthologyfilmarchives.org
Website: www.anthologyfilmarchives.org

The Anthology Film Archives is probably the finest archive in the world devoted to experimental film and video. They are not collecting Japanese works or paper materials in any concerted manner. However, because so many Japanese artists lived and worked in New York City, they do have materials that no one else has.

Arakawa Library
荒川区立図書館

Arakawa Kuritsu Toshokan
4-27-2 Arakawa
Arakawa-ku, Tokyo 116 Japan
Phone: 03-3891-4349
email: ya@library.city.arakawa.tokyo.jp
Website: www.library.city.arakawa.tokyo.jp

Anyone interested in prewar cinema will want to visit the Arakawa Library, a small public library with a precious collection of videos. Most notable are their near-full run of videos from the Tōhō Kinema Club series. This was a subscription-only series, so they are quite hard to come by. Luckily, one does not have to be a resident of Arakawa to get their library card.

Art Research Center (Ritsumeikan University)
アート•リサーチセンター

Art Research Center
Ritsumeikan University
56-1 Tōjiin Kitamachi
Kita-ku, Kyoto 603-8577 Japan
Phone: 075-466-3411
Fax: 075-466-3415
Website: www.arc.ritsumei.ac.jp

There is a lot of spadework into early cinema going on at Ritsumeikan's Art Research Center (ARC). ARC is devoted to investigating and archiving various aspects of Kyoto's art world and its history. The center has had the foresight to recognize Kyoto's central role in Japan's film history through a number of fascinating projects under Professor Tomita Mika's supervision. An industry database records the titles and local runs for thousands of films and *rensageki* in the Meiji and Taishō eras. A second project involves Makino Productions and is based on the collections of fliers, stills, newsletters, posters, and various Makino ephemera left by director Namiki Kyōtarō, cameraman Tanaka Jūzō and PR executive Tsumura Ken. A third involves similar materials from the prewar and wartime Daiei Studios, expanding the scope of the project with oral histories with former production staff. Finally, a fourth project focusses on a filmography of Onoe Matsunosuke, Japan's first great star. Significantly, these database projects involve scanning the collections (some of which are only on loan to ARC)—making a given object instantly available for on-screen study. The long-term goal is to construct interfaces between the databases. The idea is to create a supple digital system for conducting research on Kyoto's film culture. Someday, for example, one could look up the name of a given film; the industry database would reveal the theater it was shown in and on what dates; the Makino database could call up the program that was handed out in the lobby, along with press materials. At the moment, these databases are still under construction, but they are functional. They are also online, but given the complex provenance of the original materials, they will probably remain password protected for the foreseeable future. One can get a taste of the projects by visiting the ARC homepage, but only a visit to their terminals will get you the password.

Ritsumeikan's main library has a growing collection of film books and magazines, including a full run of *Kinema junpō.* ARC has cold storage and has begun acquiring films; to date, they mostly have 3,000 television commercials shot in Osaka. They even have a set of projectors once sold by Makino. Researchers with specific projects are welcome to visit the collections; however, it is essential to arrange this far ahead of time. Scans of their materials can be acquired for publication, provided copyrights are properly cleared. Finally, after your visit to ARC, do not fail to pay your respects to Makino Shōzō, Makino Masahiro, Onoe Matsunosuke, and Kinugasa Teinosuke, all of whom are buried in the nearby Tōjiin cemeteries.

Atsuta Iwanami Relational Movie Library
厚田・岩波映像資料センター

Atsuta Iwanami Eizō Shiryō Sentā
292-2 Atsuta, Atsuta-ku
Ishikari-shi, Hokkaidō 061-3601 Japan
Phone (Sapporo office): 011-622-1115
Fax (Sapporo office): 011-622-1116
email: info@a-i-kan.org
Website: www.a-i-kan.org

This small rural archive was established in 2003 through a donation of 640 prints from Iwanami, apparently because the natural climate (cold with low humidity) lends itself to cheap film preservation. They have plans to grow to a collection with several thousand prints. The building is a former primary school on the coast of the Sea of Japan, 40 kilometers from Sapporo. They are also collecting paper materials, and hold regular screenings of their films. The facility is not regularly open, so advance reservations are absolutely necessary (and a phone call may be necessary if no one answers your email).

Broadcast Library
放送ライブラリー

Hōsō Library
Yokohama Jōhō Bunka Center, 8th Floor
11 Nihon Ōdori
Naka-ku, Yokohama 231-0021 Japan
Phone: 045-222-2828
Fax: 045-641-2110
Website: www.bpcj.or.jp

A public and very easy-to-use library for television programs (both NHK and commercial television), even if its collection is not that extensive. You merely register at the entrance, search their database (which is also available online), request a program, and then you can view it at a designated television booth. (Short items like television commercials can be selected and viewed by the user at separate computers.) Their collection also contains some theatrical newsreels from the 1950s and 1960s, such as *Daimai nyūsu*.

Cartoon Library and Museum (OSU)

Cartoon Library and Museum
Ohio State University
27 West 17th Avenue Mall
Columbus, OH 43210-1393 U.S.A.
Phone: 614-292-0538
Fax: 614-292-9101
email: cartoons@osu.edu
Website: cartoons.osu.edu

With the relationship of cinema and manga becoming ever more intimate, one might want to track down the original manga of an adaptation. A number of universities libraries have begun collecting manga in specialized areas—including Cornell, Kansas, and Duke—and a quick look on WorldCat will reveal who holds what titles and is willing to lend through interlibrary loan. However, the most notable of these collections is housed at Ohio State University. Their Cartoon Library and Museum houses hundreds of thousands of original cartoons, tens of thousands of books, thousands of feet of manuscript materials, and millions of comic strip clippings. The OSU manga collection is small by comparison, but it is constantly growing and particularly important for their historical materials and limited edition reference materials. A significant number of these reference works are unavailable in Japan, where few libraries collect manga and related ephemera. In Japan, the National Diet Library (21-22) receives manga under copyright, but catalogs them poorly; the Kyoto International Manga Museum (44) associated with Kyoto Seika University will soon be the best place for research.

China Film Archive

China Film Archive
N°3, Wen Hui Yuan Road
Xiao Xi Tian, Haidian District
100082 Beijing China
Phone: 010-6225-0916/6225-0438
Fax: 010-6225-9315
email: cfafad@yahoo.com.cn

Rumor has it that the China Film Archive in Beijing holds quite a number of films and paper materials from the colonization of Manchuria and the China War era. Unfortunately, these are currently locked up and far, far from reach because of their subject matter, but the archive did acknowledge their existence when we asked. They also pointed to significant changes in the political policy regarding archival materials, hopeful shifts indicating an inclination towards openness. However, anything having to do with the war is still sensitive enough to keep it under wraps. At least they aren't throwing things away, and we can await the day when they open their vault.

Chinese Taipei Film Archive

Chinese Taipei Film Archive
Address: 4F, No. 7, Ching-tao East Road, Taipei 100, Republic of China
Tel: 886-2-2392-4243, 886-2-2396-0760
Fax: 886-2-2392-6359
email: ctfa@mail.ctfa.org.tw

Rumor has it the Chinese Taipei Film Archive holds films from the colonial era, although we were unable to confirm it.

Chōfu Shiritsu Toshokan—Eiga Shiryōshitsu
調布市立図書館 映画資料室

Chōfu Shiritsu Toshokan
2-33-1 Kojimachō
Chōfū-shi 182-0026 Japan
Phone: 042-441-6181
Fax: 042-441-6183
email: tosyokan@w2.city.chofu.tokyo.jp

Website: www.lib.city.chofu.tokyo.jp/eiga.htm

Chōfu is one of the industrial centers of the Japanese film industry thanks to the establishment of the Nikkatsu Tamagawa Studio in 1934 and Daiei's studio in 1942. The city's central library established a special collection for film in 1995, and they now have 18,000 items. This includes a number of runs of magazines, several thousand books, and many programs and shooting scripts. They also have a significant amount of industry-related documents.

Cinémathèque française

La Cinémathèque française
51, rue de Bercy, 75012 Paris, France
Phone : 01-71-19-32-00
Fax : 01-71-19-32-01
email: contact@cinematheque.fr
Website: www.cinematheque.fr
Website: www.bifi.fr (for their Bibliothèque du Film)

The Film Library of the Cinémathèque française was originally established as an independent institution in 1992, but it merged with the Cinématèque in 2007. They have about 150 books and 220 videos on Japanese cinema. They also have the personal papers of Hiroko Govaers, a central figure in the introduction of Japanese cinema to Europe. The library has a significant collection of advertising materials and other ephemera, such as posters, stills, catalogs and pamphlets. Their online catalog, the second web address above, has an excellent interface and lists all the non-film materials. It is searchable by name and/or title. Their collection is thin for Japanese language materials; however, this is the library of choice for researching in European languages (including English). They also have quite a few film prints. Inquire to see if they hold the one you require.

Cinematic Arts Library (USC)

Cinematic Arts Library
Doheny Memorial Library
University of Southern California
3550 Trousdale Parkway
Los Angeles, CA 90089-0185 U.S.A.
Phone: 213-740-3994, 213-740-8906
email: cin@usc.edu
Website: www.usc.edu/libraries/locations/cinema_tv

As a USC grad student back in the 1980s, Markus stumbled on a jewel in the Cinematic Arts Library stacks. It was a mostly complete run of the first decade of *Eiga hyōron*. Incredibly, the pages were uncut, meaning that it had never been cracked in half a century. This was probably because it had never been catalogued—and remains miscatalogued! You could say this is symptomatic. It is one of the finest film libraries in the world, but remarkably poor for Japanese film. That said, they do have a wonderful clipping file collection, with many files for Japanese directors and films. The coverage is canonical, but there are many unusual and rare items to be found in these files.

Committee for the Transmission of History
歴史伝承委員会

Committee for the Transmission of History
Rekishi Denshō Iinkai
Rinkū Building, Room 411
1-2 Goryō Bokujō, Sanrizuka
Narita-shi, Chiba 282-0011 Japan
Phone: 0476-32-2586
Fax: 0476-32-2583
email: main@rekishidensho.jp
Webpage: www.rekishidensho.jp

Strange though it may seem, a coalition of anti-airport activists and the airport authority itself teamed up to archive the famous Sanrizuka Struggle, the massive farmers' uprising that attempted to stop the construction of Narita International Airport. They call themselves the Committee for the Transmission of History, reflecting their charter to pass on the history of the struggle to future generations. To that end, they have created an archive—housed within the airport itself!—with records and objects from both sides of the conflict. Among the holdings are the Sanrizuka era collection of Ogawa Productions and the personal papers of director Fukuda Katsuhiko. The Ogawa materials are particularly extensive: 230 cans of 16mm rushes and negative, 969 reels of 6mm raw audio, 247 cassette tapes, 72 photo albums and 359 rolls of film, and 46 boxes of paper records. The latter includes phone logs, production diaries, scenarios, as well as newsletters, pamphlets, posters, and handbills from Ogawa Productions and a plethora of other social movements. The audio tapes and still photographs have all been digitized and are easy to study; they are currently transferring all the moving image material to digital video as well. The collection is open to researchers, but application is required as they have no reading room and the archive is located in a secure area of the airport. It is well worth a visit for anyone studying new left politics and independent film culture.

Diplomatic Record Office of the Ministry of Foreign Affairs
外務省外交資料館

Gaimushō Gaikō Shiryōkan
1-5-3 Azabudai
Minato-ku, Tokyo 106-0041 Japan
Phone: 03-3585-4511
Fax: 03-3585-4514
Website: www.mofa.go.jp/mofaj/annai/honsho/shiryo

Obviously, Japanese cinema is not like Hollywood; over most of its history there has been little prospect for exploiting foreign markets. This probably helps explain the paucity of records in the Ministry of Foreign Affairs' archives. Because so few Japanese films were being shown abroad, there was no reason for the ministry to intervene on the industry's behalf. The archives' film-related documents have mostly been collated into a set of binders about two feet thick. They are a motley collection of letters, cables and reports from various embassies around the globe. Most deal with either copyright infringement claims or the screenings of Japanese films in other countries. Of the latter, there are some notable traces of the famous prewar screenings in the Soviet Union.

Documentation Centre for Modern Japanese Music
日本近代音楽館

Nihon Kindai Ongakukan
1-8-14 Azabudai
Minato-ku, Tokyo 106-0041 Japan
Phone: 03-3224-1584
Fax: 03-3224-1654
Website: www.mlaj.gr.jp/members/jp/kindai.htm

The Documentation Centre for Modern Japanese Music, otherwise known as the Ongakukan, is probably the finest archive in Japan for the study of modern music. They have thousands of recordings, although this is still small compared to the National Diet Library (21-22) or the Shōwa-kan (47-48). Where the Ongakukan shines is its personal papers for over 100 composers. None of these artists were, strictly speaking, film composers on the rolls of the studios. However, so many "serious" composers (their bibliographer's term, not ours) wrote film scores that the Ongakukan deserves listing here. Composers with significant film resumes represented include Hayasaka Fumio, Takemitsu Tōru, Itō Noboru, Kami Kyōsuke, Shibata Minao, Fukai Shirō, Horiuchi Keizō, Yamada Kōsaku and others. Among these "others" is Akiyama Kunio, author of the basic history of film music, *Nihon no eiga ongakushi I* (Tokyo: Tabata Shoten, 1974). Advance notice is necessary for using these materials, and it is easiest if you contact the bibliographers with a specific name, film title, or disc title. Although the connection to Japanese cinema may be tenuous, we might as well note that Donald Richie donated a pot of Stravinsky manuscripts, letters and ephemera.

Film Preservation Society
映画保存協会

Eiga Hozon Kyōkai
5-17-3 Sendagi
Bunkyō-ku, Tokyo 113-0022 Japan
Phone/Fax: 03-3823-7633
email: info@filmpres.org
Website: www.filmpres.org

The Film Preservation Society is a non-profit group devoted to studying and conducting film preservation. They have collected and restored a number of films, which they are putting online and distributing on celluloid. Their website is a particularly good place to keep up on film preservation issues and events in Japan.

George Eastman House

George Eastman House
Motion Picture Department
900 East Avenue
Rochester, NY 14607 U.S.A.
Phone: 585-271-3361
Fax: 585-271-3970
email: film@geh.org
Website: www.eastmanhouse.org

While Eastman House is an important resource for film studies, their Japan holdings are rather small. They have about 61 films (Japanese or co-productions), about 100 items in their posters and stills collection (mainly post-1990s posters), and a handful of videos. From what we can tell, their English-subtitled print of *Wife Be Like a Rose* may be the version that opened in New York City in the 1930s. They are not quite sure, however.

Getty Research Institute

The Getty Research Institute
1200 Getty Center Drive, Suite 1100

Los Angeles, CA 90049-1688 U.S.A.
Phone: 310-440-7335
email: griweb@getty.edu
Website: www.getty.edu/research/institute/

The Getty Research Institute has just begun actively collecting experimental film and video from Japan. As of today, they have not begun cataloging their nascent collection.

Gosfilmofond of Russia

Gosfilmofond of Russia
Belye Stolby, 142050
Moskovskaja Oblast, Russia
Phone: 495-996-0520
Fax: 496-796-3498
email: gff@t50.ru
Website: www.aha.ru/~filmfond

In 1991 Markus co-programmed a retrospective on the films of World War II for the Yamagata International Documentary Film Festival. They were keen on showing films from the colonies, particularly from the Manchurian Motion Picture Association. He quickly stumbled on the rumors that many of the Man'ei movies ended up in the Soviet Union. He also hit the same brick wall that everyone else ran up against. The archives in Russia claimed they didn't have them. Then in 1993 an entrepreneurial businessman dropped in on Gosfilmofond and "discovered" them. Perhaps they had suddenly been declassified after all these years, or maybe the man at the front desk just didn't know he was supposed to keep the films hidden, but probably they simply smelled money. The businessman brought all 300 reels back and began selling them through his company Ten Sharp; he even refused to show the tapes to researchers unless they purchased the incredibly expensive set. The original films are still at Gosfilmofond. A sense for what the films are like may be gleaned from the heavily illustrated *Manshū no kiroku* (Tokyo: Shūeisha, 1995). Russian archives also house other Japanese films, which the National Film Center has been checking and, when possible, repatriating.

Hashima Movie Museum
羽島市映画資料館

Hashima-shi Eiga Shiryōkan
2624-1 Takehana-chō, Hashima-shi
Gifu 501-6241 Japan
Phone: 058-391-2234

Fax: 058-391-7663
email: rekimin@ccn3.aitai.ne.jp
Website: www.hashima-rekimin.jp

Back in the Taishō and early Shōwa eras, rural Hashima was home to something like seven movie theaters. One of the largest, and by far the longest surviving, was the Takehana Asahi Theater. It was constructed in 1931 and went out of business in 1971. After housing an unrelated business for many years, the owner decided to tear it down. However, a citizen's movement appeared to save this last vestige of local film culture. Unfortunately, the building had passed the point of no return, and they determined it was impossible to repair. The city tore it down and built a new building based on the original theater's design (combined with elements of a castle that sat on the same spot centuries before). Before destroying the building, the movement discovered 5,000 posters inside. This became the core of a poster collection housed in the new building. When news spread of this new poster-centered library, donations poured in. Today, a theater in Gifu regularly sends them posters and handbills to keep their collection up-to-date and ever-growing. In 2008 they held 24,196 posters for 8,000 film titles, 441 lobby stands, 36,127 handbills, 951 pamphlets, 2,660 press sheets, and 21,024 still photographs. These materials are fully catalogued, although researchers or museum curators interested in seeing them should contact the library with specific requests long ahead of time. A space on the second floor houses some curiosities from the original theater: tickets, projectors, umbrellas, and even *hibachi.* In addition to this they display thematic arrays of posters, sprinkled among objects advertising the latest films in theaters.

Hibiya Public Library
日比谷図書館

Tokyo Metropolitan Hibiya Public Library
Hibya Toshokan
1-4 Hibiya Kōen
Chiyoda-ku, Tokyo 100-0012 Japan
Phone: 03-3502-0101
Website: www.library.metro.tokyo.jp
Copies: service costs 25 yen a page, and can be ordered from throughout Japan; digital cameras can be used.

For a public library, Hibiya has a significant collection of both film books (1,140 volumes, but only two magazines) and videos (310), but the main feature is the 16mm print collection. The library has amassed 9,399 films, and most of them can be checked out along with projectors. Hibiya also houses 21,000 music recordings (including CDs), 4,400 audio-tapes, and 2,700 slide films. They created a public index of the films: *Eiga mokuroku 1999-nen* (140), one example of a genre of indexes published by postwar public libraries. This is made somewhat superfluous by the up-to-date database on their website, although this is missing nearly 1,000 titles; because they are a lending library, the online catalog has only films cleared for public performance. The films are primarily documentaries, with many canonical films represented. There are 350 works from Iwanami alone, in addition to important works by Tsuchimoto Noriaki, Ogawa Shinsuke and other famous directors.

Hiroshima City Cinematographic and Audio-Visual Library
広島市映像文化ライブラリー

Hiroshima-shi Eizō Bunka Raiburarī
3-1 Moto-machi
Naka-ku, Hiroshima 730-0011 Japan
Phone: 082-223-3525
Fax 082-228-0312
email: eizou@cf.city.hiroshima.jp
Website: www.cf.city.hiroshima.jp/eizou/

The Hiroshima City Cinematographic and Audio-Visual Library is primarily a film archive. They have no paper materials available for research, although what little they do have sometimes goes on display for public exhibitions. Established in 1982, this was probably the first local film archive to open in Japan. It retains this local charter, lending films, tapes and projectors to local non-profit groups and schools at no charge. A partial list of their documentary videos and 16mm films can be found on the website, and is broken down into genre. Their strengths are on older, independent animation and, naturally, films connected to the peace movement. The collection is of modest size: 545 35mm films, 1,878 16mm films, 241 8mm films, all of which are catalogued in a paper index. There are also 3,693 videos, nearly 500 of which are Japanese productions. The public is welcome to view videos and listen to audio recordings without reservations. They charge an insignificant usage fee for this. A small, 24-seat preview room may be used for screening 16mm prints; reservations and a ¥1,810/hour fee are required. Unfortunately, they use their 169-seat 35mm room for public screenings so the 35mm prints are out of reach.

Hōsei University Institute for Okinawa Studies
法政大学沖縄文化研究所

Hōsei Daigaku Okinawa Bunka Kenkyūjo
2-17-1 Fujimi

Chiyoda-ku, Tokyo 102-8160
Phone: 03-3264-9393
Fax: 03-3264-9335
email: okiken@s-adm.hosei.ac.jp
Website: www.hosei.ac.jp/fujimi/okiken

With around 100 videos on Okinawa, this is a convenient option for studying up on Okinawan film if a trip to Naha is out of the question. Their book and periodical collection is substantial (over 20,000 volumes).

Ichikawa Literature Plaza
市川市文学プラザ

Ichikawa-shi Bungaku Puraza
1-1-4 Onitaka, Ichikawa-shi
Chiba 272-8501 Japan
Phone: 047-320-3354
Fax: 047-320-3354
Website: www.city.ichikawa.lg.jp/cul01/bunpla.html

After the 2003 death of screenwriter Mizuki Yōko, Ichikawa City received a donation of her library amounting to more than 100 boxes of scripts, manuscripts, scrapbooks and letters. Mizuki wrote many of the great films of the 1950s, and this wonderful collection—catalogued by a group of local volunteers—is already seeing visits by serious researchers.

Ikeda Bunko Library
池田文庫

Ikeda Bunko
12-1 Sakaehonmachi, Ikeda-shi
Osaka-fu 563-0058
Phone: 072-751-3185
Fax: 072-751-3302
email: ikedabunko@gaea.ocn.ne.jp
Website: www.ikedabunko.or.jp

The Ikeda Bunko Library (110,000 volumes) was founded by the owner of Hankyū railways and the Takarazuka theater troupe as the Takarazuka Bungei Toshokan. The name changed to Ikeda Bunko Library after the war. It specializes in performing arts, including cinema. There are approximately 1,700 books, 11,000 magazine numbers, and 400 scenarios in their film holdings (the latter are mostly from the Takarazuka Film Studio [1951-1968]).

They also have a small amount of ephemera, such as still photographs and programs. There is no online catalog; however, some sense for their wartime holdings may be gleaned from their old newsletter, the *Takarazuka bungei toshokan geppō* (which has been reprinted in Makino Mamoru's *Kindai eiga engeki ongaku shoshi*). The entire library of their previous incarnation is preserved as a separate and coherent special collection. Access is free, although not to the stacks. Some of their more precious materials require both prior reservations and letters of introduction, but most of the film materials are immediately available for perusal.

Imperial War Museum

Imperial War Museum
Lambeth Road
London SE1 6HZ
United Kingdom
Phone: 020-7416-5320
Fax: 020-7416-5374
email: mail@iwm.org.uk
Website: www.iwm.org.uk

The Imperial War Museum has a massive collection of films, perhaps over 50,000 prints. They do have an online database, but it only wets the appetite. Depending on the collection, the cataloging is incomplete. Quite a few Japanese propaganda films from the war come up, but they often refer to records that do not appear to be online. Unfortunately, one cannot search and browse by record group. It's likely a visit is in order for anyone writing about the war period.

Japan Center for Asian Historical Records
アジア歴史資料センター

Ajia Rekishi Shiryō Sentā
National Archives of Japan
4th fl., Sumitomo Hanzomon Bldg., Annex
2-1-2 Hirakawachō
Chiyoda-ku, Tokyo 102-0093 Japan
Phone: 03-3556-8801
Fax: 03-3261-1521
Website: www.jacar.go.jp

While the Center has a physical address, it is mostly a virtual institution nominally within the National Archives of Japan (46). One could visit them, but their reading room has only computer terminals with the same database available on the internet. This database combines documents relating to Japan and its relationship to Asia, documents that are held by The National Archives of Japan (46), The Diplomatic Record Office of the Ministry of Foreign Affairs (36), and The National Institute for Defense Studies of the Ministry of Defense. They cover the period from Meiji to the end of WWII. The documents are all scanned, and viewable at home with a browser plug-in.

There are a wide variety of records about cinema, although the number is less than one might imagine; a search for *"eiga"* comes up with just short of a thousand hits on everything from censorship policy discussion to drafts of the 1939 Film Law. Presumably, the relatively small size of this document cache has something to do with the historical lack of openness regarding government records, as well as the fiery fate of so much of the archive during (and immediately after) WWII. However, the very existence of this online database signals a shift in the government's stance, and promises more riches for researchers in the future.

Korean Film Archive

Korean Film Archive
1602 DMC, Sangam-dong, Mapo-gu
Seoul, Korea 120-270
Phone: 02-3153-2001
Fax: 02-3153-2080
Website: www.koreafilm.or.kr

By the archive's count, none of the 68 colonial films made before 1930 are extant; and of the 231 pre-1950 films, only 19 remain in the vaults. You can see which ones via their online database.

Kyoto City International Foundation
京都市国際交流協会

Kyoto City Kokusai Kōryū Kyōkai
2-1 Torii-chō, Awataguchi
Sakyō-ku, Kyoto 606-8536 Japan
Phone: 075-752-3010
Fax: 075-752-3510
email: office@kcif.or.jp
Website: www.kcif.or.jp/en

The library at the Kyoto City International Foundation has several hundred commercial videos. It is a good resource for anyone living in Kyoto.

Kyoto International Manga Museum
京都国際マンガミュージアム

Kyōto Kokusai Manga Myūjiamu
Karasuma-Oike
Nakagyō-ku, Kyoto 604-0846 Japan
Phone: 075-254-7414
Fax: 075-254-7424
email: via web form
Website: www.kyotomm.com/international/english

There are manga museums scattered all across Japan, such as the Contemporary Manga Library Naiki Collection in Tokyo, but this is associated with Kyoto Seika University's programs on manga and animation and is clearly the best of the bunch. Housed in a beautifully renovated primary school, the Kyoto International Manga Museum greets the visitor with an expanse of artificial turf in the heart of Kyoto. There is a permanent collection, rotating special exhibits and literally tens of thousands of manga adorning the walls. This is one museum where one is encouraged to touch the art.

The museum has a research room were one can order and read manga from their closed stacks and their budding collection of personal papers. Although they only just opened, they have amassed a collection of over 200,000 items. This figure grows by the day, as they seem to be getting more donations than they know what to do with. At the time of publication, they were still trying to decide what degree of access to grant to researchers.

Mainichi Eigasha
毎日映画社

Mainichi Eigasha
1-1-1 Hitotsubashi
Chiyoda-ku, Tokyo 100-0003 Japan
Phone: 03-3212-0751
Fax: 03-3214-2966
email: mic.tokyo@mainichieiga.co.jp
Website: www.mainichieiga.co.jp

The *Mainichi shinbun* newspaper has had a film unit since at least 1930. They were one of the first companies to produce long-form documentaries, but most of their output was in the form of newsreels. From the looks of their website, they now seem to put more energy into creating a motion picture record of the imperial family. Their website also has an index of the films in their library. Mainichi also owns the rights to *Nikkatsu sekai nyūsu*, and has a separate website devoted just to that newsreel (www.mbs.jp/nikkatsu).

Margaret Herrick Library

Margaret Herrick Library
Academy of Motion Picture Arts and Sciences
Fairbanks Center for Motion Picture Study
333 S. La Cienega Boulevard
Beverly Hills, CA 90211 U.S.A.
Phone: 310-247-3020
Fax: 310-657-5193
email: via web form
Website: www.oscars.org/mhl/index.html

The Margaret Herrick Library has a few resources of interest. They have a nearly complete collection of English-language publications on Japanese cinema. Their poster collection has quite a few examples of domestic and foreign posters for Japanese releases, and the searchable database generally includes scans of the posters. The papers of producer Elmo Williams tell the inside story of Kurosawa Akira's disastrous experience on the *Tora! Tora! Tora!* set. And as the archive of the Academy of Motion Picture Arts and Sciences, they have paper and audio-visual records from the events surrounding every year's Oscars and the visits of Japanese artists like Kurosawa. Finally, their website also has a powerful database for the script holdings of six Los Angeles area archives and libraries; these are deep collections and contain quite a few translations of Japanese scripts.

Museum of Modern Art

Celeste Bartos International Film Study Center
MoMA
11 West 53 Street
New York, NY 10019-5497 U.S.A.
Phone: 212-708-9613
e-mail: fsc@moma.org
Website: www.moma.org

The Celeste Bartos International Film Study Center is the researcher's interface with the Museum of Modern Art's wonderful collection of screenplays, clipping files, books, periodicals, and special collections of all sorts. There are also, of course, many films, and the Center is generally able to accommodate requests for viewing, providing one gives them at least two weeks notice. They also have records and recordings of past MoMA events.

National Archives of Japan
国立公文書館

Kokuritsu Kōbunshokan
3-2 Kitanomaru Kōen
Chiyoda-ku, Tokyo 102-0091 Japan
Phone: 03-3214-0621
Fax: 03-3212-8806
Website: www.archives.go.jp

In comparison to NARA (19-21), the diminutive size of the building and staff of the National Archives of Japan evidences the Japanese government's disinterest in the official archive. It does have a handful of records on cinema (use search terms like *"eiga," "katsudō shashin,"* and *"firumu"*). Their catalog is online, and has documents that do not show up in the Japan Center for Asian Historical Records database (42). Their holdings cover all sorts of areas, and few with any depth. One never knows what will show up, so anyone studying government policy, censorship, propaganda and other themes should pay their website a visit. Searches list documents that are either "Open" or "Require Examination." In the former case, a surprising number of documents have been scanned, as indicated by a "Browse" button that will immediately call up the document in a new window. Records that "require examination" are available at the tail end of a bureaucratic process that may or may not yield favorable results. Basically, one fills out a request and hopes for the best. On the other hand, "Open" documents or microfilms are delivered to the reading room in short order, if a scan is not instantly available online.

National Institute for Education Policy Research Education Library
国立教育政策研究所　教育図書館

Kyōiku Toshokan
National Institute for Educational Policy Research of Japan
3-2-2 Kasumigaseki
Chiyoda-ku, Tokyo 100-8951 Japan
Phone: 03-6733-6536
Fax: 03-6733-6957
email: library@nier.go.jp
Website: www.nier.go.jp/library/index.html

For educational films and the Ministry of Education's involvement in the film world, The Education Library is a central resource. At the heart of this subject area is the Nakada Shunzō Collection. Nakada was a ministry bureaucrat dealing with film in the prewar and wartime eras. His papers include 570 volumes, along with some unique materials totalling 65 items. This library is rather difficult to use. The main obstacle is their requirement that one applies for entry at least a week beforehand (see the website for details).

The National Museum of Ethnology
国立民族学博物館

Kokuritsu Minzokugaku Hakubutsukan
10-1 Senri Expo Park, Suita-shi
Osaka 565-8511 Japan
Phone: 06-6876-2151
Fax: 06-6875-0401
email: staff@minpaku.ac.jp
Website: www.minpaku.ac.jp

The library of the museum contains one of the best film book collections in the country, at more than 2,500 volumes.

National Shōwa Memorial Museum (Shōwa-kan)
昭和館

National Shōwa Memorial Museum
Shōwa-kan Sōmubu
1-6-1 Kudan Minami
Chiyoda-ku, Tokyo 102-0074 Japan
Phone: 03-3222-2577
Fax: 03-3222-2575
Website: www.showakan.go.jp
Entrance Fee: ¥300

Located just down the street from the infamous Yasukuni Shine, the Shōwa-kan was established in 1997 to commemorate the life of Japanese people before, during, and after World War II. You have to pay to see the exhibits on the sixth and seventh floors, but the visual and sound library on the fifth floor is free. There you can search and view a variety of visual and sound materials on fourteen computer screens. There are over 1,500 films from the early 1930s to the 1960s, more than two thirds of which are newsreels from the major producers: Asahi, Yomiuri, Mainichi and *Nihon nyūsu*. There are also other feature-length and short documentaries, plus some home movies. You can search by year, category and keyword. Their digital library also contains photos, popular music and the full text of several magazines. This is a particularly convenient place to watch films from around World War II. We should also point out the enormous Maekawa Collection of sound recordings. These 30,000+ discs include nearly everything issued on 78s in the prewar era and many in other formats. This naturally includes a lot of film music, as well as *benshi* recordings. The SP records are indexed in the fat *SP rekōdo 60,000-kyoku sōmokuroku* (Tokyo: Atene Shobō, 2003).

Netherlands Filmmuseum

Het Filmmuseum
Vondelstraat 69 / 71
1054 GK Amsterdam, Netherlands
Phone: 020-589-1435
Fax: 020-589-1454
email: info@filmmuseum.nl
Website: www.filmmuseum.nl

The Netherlands Filmmuseum and its library has a solid collection of books and periodicals on Japan, primarily in European languages. These may be searched ahead of time on their website's database. The archives hold just over 200 Japanese films. Most of these are from the war and beyond, and about a fourth of them are readily viewable on video. An unusual aspect of their library collection are hundreds of scenarios, often the product of the subtitling process. Copying is possible, and the library may be able to accommodate researchers outside of the hours they are open to the general public.

Netherlands Institute for Sound and Vision

The Netherlands Institute of Sound and Vision
Media Park, Sumatralaan 45
PO Box 1060
1200 BB Hilversum, Netherlands
Phone: 035-677-3434
email: klantenservice@beeldengeluid.nl
Website: www.beeldengeluid.nl

The Netherlands Institute for Sound and Vision is an important repository for prints of films made during the Japanese occupation of the Dutch East Indies.

Netherlands Institute for War Documentation

Netherlands Institute for War Documentation
Herengracht 380

1016 JC Amsterdam, Netherlands
Phone: 020-523-3800
Fax: 020-523-3888
email: info@niod.nl
Website: www.niod.nl

This archive preserves materials from WWII and other conflicts. They have a handful of Japanese videos, but whatever film prints they acquired are held by the Netherlands Institute for Sound and Vision (see above). We hear that they do, however, have some very unusual paper materials regarding the film industry in the Japanese-occupied Dutch East Indies.

NHK Archives
NHKアーカイブス

NHK Archives
Skip City
3-12-63 Kamiaoki
Kawaguchi-shi, Saitama 333-0844 Japan
Phone: 048-268-8000
Website: www.nhk.or.jp/archives

In the early 2000s, NHK set up viewing booths in the lobbies of their local offices across Japan. Each booth is connected to the NHK Archives in Saitama Prefecture, which serves up the films upon request. The website's database has records of varying quality for 300,000 television and radio programs. There is a separate database for the 6,000 programs one can actually view online. Although this is a spectacular resource for studying the history of Japanese broadcasting, not to mention contemporary history itself, every branch we have visited was virtually empty except for the stray senior citizen passing the days in rapt nostalgia. There are short samples of a few hundred programs available through the internet, certainly a promising indication of where this massive archive is heading.

Nihon University College of Art Library
日本大学藝術学部図書館

Nihon Daigaku Geijutsu Gakubu Toshokan
2-42-1 Asahigaoka
Nerima-ku, Tokyo 176-8525 Japan
Tel: 03-5995-8336
email: library@art.nihon-u.ac.jp
Website: www.art.nihon-u.ac.jp/facilities/library

Having one of the oldest programs teaching film studies and production in Japan (since 1929!), and having major historians like Tanaka Jun'ichirō once serve on the faculty, the Geijutsu Gakubu features a significant collection of film-related materials in its library. The copy of *Katsudō shashinkai* used for the Kokusho Kankōkai reprint, for instance, was the Nichidai copy. While it does not have major personal collections like the Waseda Tsubouchi Theater Museum or the National Film Center, there are some magazines and monographs here that are not easily found elsewhere. The library used to be open to the general public, but as with many other Japanese university libraries, it now requires a letter of introduction from your university if you don't have a Nichidai ID. At the time of this writing, the entire College of Art campus is being rebuilt, so it is not yet certain what the library will be like when construction is complete, especially how the collection will be divided between the Ekota Campus and the Tokorozawa Campus branches. We recommend you check online, or contact the library directly, before trying to use it.

Ōhara Institute for Social Research
法政大学大原社会問題研究所

Hōsei Daigaku Ōhara Shakai Mondai Kenkyūjo
Hōsei University
4342 Aiharamachi, Machida-shi
Tokyo 194-0298 Japan
Phone: 042-783-2307
Fax: 042-783-2311
email: oharains@s-adm.hosei.ac.jp
Website: oohara.mt.tama.hosei.ac.jp/english/index.html

Created in 1909, this is the oldest research institute devoted to labor and social movements. It became part of Hōsei University in 1949, and now has a significant number of resources on the web. They have several online databases with thousands of posters and photographs, hundreds of which are related to films, film-related strikes, and screenings. The library holds many books about labor actions and union activities in the film world. There are also many unique collections of materials from the police, unions, and other political groups. Most of Ōhara's film materials are scattered throughout the archive; however, there are a few shelves worth noting. Leftist organizations seem to naturally network each other, so a given file tends to have fascinating pamphlets, posters, newsletters, and fliers from a wide variety of unions, local movements and strikes. This is the kind of material preserved in the collections centered on Sōhyō's Kokumin Bunka Kaigi and the Nihon Eiga Engeki Rōdō Kumiai. Ōhara also has a few classic videos from the postwar independent film movement, as well as film prints of some of the first activist films from late Taishō and early Shōwa. Finally, they have a fine collection of documents relating to the Tōhō strike. Ōhara is an open and hospitable library and, while it may require serious spade-work to get to its riches, it is an important resource for anyone studying leftist filmmaking in Japan.

Okinawa Prefectural Archives
沖縄県公文書館

Okinawa Kōbunshokan
148-3 Arakawa, Haebaru-chō
Shimajiri-gun, Okinawa 901-1105 Japan
Phone: 098-888-3875
Fax: 098-888-3879
Website: www.archives.pref.okinawa.jp

A citizen's movement called the 10-Fīto Undō initiated the repatriation of wartime film from NARA, using donations to purchase ten feet of film at a time. More formal and complete work was undertaken by the Okinawa Prefectural Archives, the best place to view films shot in the islands. Their collection is mostly catalogued and searchable online. Films can easily be seen on site, but some are available for copying and still others are streaming off their website. See (141) the introductions to their collection.

Onomichi Eiga Shiryōkan
おのみち映画資料館

Onomichi Eiga Shiryōkan
1-14-10 Kubō, Onomichi-shi
Hiroshima 722-0045 Japan
Phone: 0848-37-8141
Website: www.bbbn.jp/~eiga2000
Entrance Fee: ¥500

Tucked under some stairs, this could be the smallest film library in Japan. This is why we couldn't resist including it in this book. It is more of a museum dedicated to some of the local film history, most particularly the visits by Ozu Yasujirō and Shindō Kaneto.

Osaka Prefectural Library
大阪府立図書館

Osaka Furitsu Chūō Toshokan

1-2-1 Aramoto-kita
Higashi Osaka-shi 577-0011 Japan
Phone: 06-6745-0170

Osaka Furitsu Nakanoshima Toshokan
1-2-10 Nakanoshima
Kita-ku, Osaka 530-0005 Japan
Phone: 06-6203-0474
Website: 210.167.252.45/central/english.html

This is another large collection of film books (over 4,000) split between the central library and the beautiful Nakanoshima branch. Check the online catalog beforehand to find out which library has the volume you're looking for. They also have videos.

Ōta City Nitta Library
太田市立新田図書館

Ōta Shiritsu Nitta Toshokan
877 Nitta Sorimachi-chō
Ōta-shi, Gunma 370-0313 Japan
Phone: 0276-57-2676
Fax: 0276-57-2677
Webpage: www.lib.ota.gunma.jp/nitta/index.html

Tanaka Jun'ichirō was once head of *Kinema junpō* and author of the massive *Nihon eiga hattatsushi* (131-132). While previous editors of *KineJun* came from the salon and thus wrote from their gut, Tanaka had a bent toward industrial history and based his writing on research, interviews, and the constant collection of materials. He donated his personal collection to the library in his home town of Nitta. The library celebrated this gift and Tanaka's life work in a series of festivals, accompanied by a set of six thick catalogs (76). The collection itself is fully catalogued on a searchable database at the library. The books and a list of still photographs can be found in the out-of-print *Tanaka Jun'ichirō eiga shiryō katsuyō chōsa kenkyū* (Nitta-chō: Nitta Chōritsu Toshokan, 1991). The core of the collection includes 479 books and a few magazine runs, most of which are held in more accessible libraries. The main attractions for researchers outside of Gunma are the carefully catalogued and preserved still photographs of actors and directors and Tanaka's wonderful scrapbooks. The stills are mostly from the prewar era, and the library is willing to reproduce them for publication providing the author takes responsibility for clearing all rights. Tanaka began the 18 scrapbooks in 1917 at the age of 15, just two years after seeing his first film. They are newspaper clippings organized both by year and theme, running into the early Shōwa period. Reading *Nihon eiga hattatsushi,* you would expect to find a mountain of unique materials, as Tanaka quotes liberally from all manner of print matter and personal interviews. However, the collection is surprisingly small. This seems to be because before his death, he allowed Satō Tadao to comb his library for resources that would enable the research for Satō's own multivolume history of Japanese cinema (131).

Ōya Sōichi Library
大宅壮一文庫

Ōya Sōichi Bunko
3-10-20 Hachimanyama
Setagaya-ku, Tokyo 156-0056 Japan
Phone: 03-3303-2000
Website: www.oya-bunko.or.jp
Entrance Fee: ¥500 per 10 articles, ¥300 for students with letter of introduction

This is the finest collection of popular periodicals from the Meiji Era to the present. The only film specialty magazine they are cataloging is *Kinema junpō,* but their other magazines are an essential resource for looking at the gossipy side of film culture. Their catalog takes three forms: paper, CD-ROM, and online database—each rising steeply in price and thus corresponding to their availability. The online database is generally not found outside of Japanese research universities, but the books are widely available. This is a wonderful resource, but it is important to note that the coverage of their index is increasingly spotty the further you go back in time. Relatively complete indexing of *KineJun* only begins in 1986. They do, however, keep a complete bound and xeroxed copy of the *KineJun* table of contents for the entire postwar run, a resource you can also find in the Waseda reference room. There are many rules and fees for using the Ōya Sōichi Library, so it is best to study up before your visit by reading the website. They allow photography, but only by appointment and it costs more than photocopies.

Sterling Memorial Library (Yale University)

Sterling Memorial Library
Yale University
130 Wall Street
New Haven, CT 06511 U.S.A.
Phone: 203-432-1775
email: smlref@yale.edu
Website: www.library.yale.edu

Beyond its significant collection of Japanese film-related books and magazines,

Yale has begun actively collecting printed ephemera, especially theater programs, handbills, and pressbooks. Although the first portions are still at the cataloging stage, the collection continues to expand, and will eventually be made available in Manuscripts and Archives within Sterling Memorial Library. A finding aid will allow users to search the contents online. Original items cannot be checked out or made available through inter-library loan, although copies can be made of items that are not too delicate. The current collection features programs or handbills from nearly 1,000 films, weighted towards works after 1980.

Tainan National University of the Arts

Tainan National University of the Arts
No.66, Daci Village, Guantian Township
Tainan County, Taiwan 72045
Website: www.tnnua.edu.tw

Has 168 colonial-era films acquired from an antiques collector in 2003, and restored under a program funded by the National Museum of Taiwan History. They were accompanied by 135 film licenses, which provide quite a bit of information about the films and how they were used.

Tokyo Metropolitan Central Library
東京都立中央図書館

Tokyo Toritsu Chūō Toshokan
5-7-13 Minami Azabu,
Minato-ku, Tokyo 106-8575 Japan
Phone: 03-3442-8451
Fax: 03-3447-8924
email: ref-diff@library.metro.tokyo.jp
Website: www.library.metro.tokyo.jp

This branch of the Tokyo Library also has a collection similar to, though smaller than, that of the Hibiya branch (39-40).

Tokyo Metropolitan Museum of Photography Library
東京都写真美術館

Tokyo-to Shashin Bijutsukan
1-13-3 Mita
Meguro-ku, Tokyo 153-0062 Japan
Phone: 03-3280-0099

Fax: 03-3280-0033
Webpage: www.syabi.com

The Tokyo Metropolitan Museum of Photography has a small reading room interfacing with its collection, which is bifurcated into two sections that do not interact well. One half is the library, which has a relatively small collection of books and magazines. These include some publications on cinema but, not surprisingly, most are on still photography. There is an online catalog for these printed materials. The other half is the museum's extensive collection of still photography. There is a visual database for this collection in the library, and while they do not seem to be collecting publicity stills and other cinema-related genres of still photography, they do have fine examples of zoetropes, phenakistoscopes, and other pre-cinema toys, as well as original prints from Muybridge and Marey. Unfortunately, the rules they have set up for looking at their archival materials make the collection virtually impossible to use for researchers not residing in Japan. The database is not online, so one must conduct searches of their holdings in the library; only a few items can be ordered at a time, and this must be done two weeks ahead of time. Do the math and you can see the problem. There is also a charge for viewing objects.

Tōei Movieland Library
東映太秦映画村　映画資料室

Tōei Uzumasa Eigamura Eiga Shiryōshitsu
10 Higashihachigaoka-chō, Uzumasa
Ukyo-ku, Kyoto 616-8586 Japan
Phone: 075-864-7718
Website: www.eigamura30.com

The section of Kyoto called Uzumasa began its relationship with cinema when Bantsuma (Bandō Tsumasaburō) located his studio there in 1925. Over the years, quite a few studios established lots there; however, since the downturn of the 1960s, only Tōei and Kyōto Eiga Satsueijo (formerly Shōchiku's local studio) remain. Tōei avoided the fate of the others by converting its studio into a theme park in 1975. Today it is both a theme park and a working studio for period films and television shows. Check their website before you go, and you can schedule your visit during one of the shootings.

At the beginning of this venture, the theme park was sufficiently rich enough to establish an archive. This initial period of accumulation forms the core of their collection. They have close to full runs of *Kinema junpō, Eiga hyōron* and a nice collection of books. All are available for perusal, although the workspace is limited.

The main feature of this library is the extremely large and complete collection of advertising materials for nearly all mainstream films after 1975. Additionally, they have some very unusual production, post-production and exhibition records for Tōei films. Their database is up-to-date (although the software is antique). Request a given film title, and they can immediately tell you the extent of their holdings. Copies of visual materials (advertisements from the press kits, stills, posters, etc.) may be purchased, but clearing the rights is the responsibility of the author and publisher. They also have a set of photo albums with images from the early days of cinema. That these particular photos show up in book after book is probably evidence that Tōei is one of the most convenient sources for film stills in Japan.

They do not have any films, although there is a middle-sized collection of video tapes of films broadcast on television, including the dubbed versions of foreign films. These include films which have yet to be released on home video. Finally, do not miss Movieland's Eiga Bunkakan. Although the theme park is rather cheesy, the Bunkakan is not. They have nice displays on filmmaking in Kyoto, some of which indicate where one can find former studios and the graves of famous film figures. Since Movieland's establishment, Tōei has given a lifetime achievement award to a filmmaker every year. Each awardee has a large case in the Bunkakan where one can see everything from a handwritten Itami Mansaku scenario to Kurosawa Akira's captain's cap.

Toyota City Museum of Local History
豊田市郷土資料館

Toyota Kyōdo Shiryōkan
1-21 Jinnaka-chō
Toyota-shi, Aichi 471-0079 Japan
Phone: 0565-32-6561
Fax: 0565-34-0095
email: info@toyota-rekihaku.com
Website: www.toyota-rekihaku.com

Local collector Tada Toshikatsu donated the papers of director Kanemori Banshō to this local museum. Kanemori was a director for Makino Shōzō, and the collection includes his diaries, letters from Makino, press-related materials, scenarios, pre-production documents such as costume designs, snapshots from the sets of Makino's productions, and assorted curiosities (subtitle cards, Kanemori's glasses, etc.). Access to the collection is open, and the museum is willing to help with reproductions for publication; however, they do require advance notice for any visits. An index of the collection may be found at the end of an exhibition catalog they produced: *Makino Eiga no jidai: Toyota-shi Kyōdo Shiryōkan shozō eiga shiryō mokuroku* (Toyota: Toyota-shi Kyōiku Iinkai, 1996).

Yamagata Documentary Film Library
山形ドキュメンタリーフィルムライブラリー

Yamagata Documentary Film Library
100 Hirakubo, Yamagata-shi
Yamagata 990-0076 Japan
Phone: 023-635-3015
Fax: 023-635-3030
email: info@yidff.jp
Website: www.yidff.jp/library/library-e.html

The Yamagata International Documentary Film Festival is the premier venue for nonfiction film in Asia. While the festival is held biennially, it does run a film library that is open year-round. The library welcomes researchers, who will find a deep collection on the documentary form. There are some books and magazines, but the main attraction here is the video and film collection. The festival's entry form provides for the acquisition of videos submitted for the competition. Thus, the library grows by the thousands after every festival. Because of this unusual acquisition strategy, its collection represents a fair snapshot of world documentary since the first event in 1989. Furthermore, any film that showed in the competition section is available on film (for works based on celluloid), as the festival purchases prints for subtitling and distribution. The YIDFF is also known for the rigor of its retrospectives, and some of these films are also represented in the collection on both video and celluloid. There are five video booths and a 40-seat theater (16mm & 35mm) available for viewing prints.

Yamanashi Prefectural Library
山梨県立図書館

Yamanashi Kenritsu Toshokan
2-33-1 Marunouchi, Kōfu-shi
Yamanashi 400-0031 Japan
Phone: 055-226-2586
Fax: 055-226-2528
email: ken-tosho@lib.pref.yamanashi.jp
Website: www.lib.pref.yamanashi.jp

This prefectural library acquired the rich personal collection of *benshi* Umemura Shisei. Umemura began his career at the Asakusa Kinema Club in 1917, and subsequently worked at the Teikokukan, Denkikan, Kanda Kinema and other famous theaters. This collection includes 2,000 books and 5,000 magazine issues (which are still being cataloged at this point, but nearly done). Among the books are several dozen scenarios. There would have been far more in the collection had he not lost most everything in the 1923 earthquake. Most of what's left is listed up in *Umemura Shisei bunko mokuroku* (Kōfu: Yamanashi Kenritsu Toshokan, 1987), which is also available in the reference room of the Diet Library (21-22). This index does specify the numbers of periodicals in the collection, some of which are very unusual. Umemura's donation also included clipping albums, letters, and notebooks; incredibly, the library has decided not to make them public, reasoning that these were of a private nature. Thus, they sit on the unique archive of a *benshi,* who presumably now rolls in his grave.

Yūbari Kinema-kan
夕張キネマ館

Yūbari Kinema-kan
7 Takamatsu, Yūbarishi
Hokkaido 068-0401 Japan
Phone: 0123-52-3456
Fax: 0123-52-1611
Website: www.yubari-resort.com/green/facility/cinema.php

The Yūbari Kinema-kan is embedded in Yūbari Resort, a local strategy to deal with the economic woes of this old coal mining town. It was established in 2003. The core of the collection was a gift of 25,000 posters for both domestic and foreign films. They also have other kinds of ephemera and runs of major film magazines. One probably wouldn't make a special trip here, unless of course it were for the wonderful Yūbari Fantastic Film Festival—or if you were looking for posters or studying local exhibition.

II. Distributors

Needless to say, the era of 16mm and 35mm rental is almost over. Our Japanese cinema film series at the University of Michigan and Yale have become increasingly dependent on prints from Japan over the last decade. Screenings of film on film have become the domain of international film festivals, museums, archives, and rich universities. While the number of distributors decreases, it remains relatively easy to show films—depending on one's budget and facilities. Archives and museums can access the National Film Center through FIAF. The rest of us usually use some combination of the Japan Foundation (see below), Janus (which has a lot of Ozu, Kurosawa and Mizoguchi), Matsuda Film Productions (17-18), the Kawakita Memorial Film Institute (12-13) and the Kōbe Planet Film Archive (15-16). Independent filmmakers usually have their own prints and are more than happy to rent them out; their contact information is usually available through the Eiga nenkan *(85), the Green Book (103), the National Film Center, Kawakita, and the Japan Foundation, or one of the film festivals. When a recent Japanese film gets picked up by a foreign distributor, the contact can generally be found by searching the websites of local international film festivals that screened the film. You can occassionally find a distributor of a recent film through the IMDB (151), especially the Pro version. Finally, another strategy some people use is posting an inquiry to KineJapan (152-153), drawing on the networks of the list's 700 members.*

The Best

Japan Foundation
国際交流基金

Film, TV, and Publication Division
Japan Foundation/Kokusai Kōryū Kikin
4-4-1 Yotsuya, Shinjuku-ku
Tokyo 160-0004 Japan
Phone: 03-5369-6064
Fax: 03-5369-6038
email: Film_TV_and_Publication_Division@jpf.go.jp
Website: www.jpf.go.jp

Thank goodness for the Japan Foundation. As the market for 16mm film distribution dries up, this independent administrative agency devoted to cultural exchange has become one of the few places to find prints of Japanese films.

Japan Foundation has collected subtitled prints since its establishment in 1972, beginning with cultural documentaries. The Tokyo office has 550 35mm films and 1,200 documentaries (1,000 of these are feature films). The branches scattered around the world have small video libraries (with online lists at their websites), and a select number keep an additional 2,670 prints, usually in the local languages. These include cultural films in Budapest, Kuala Lumpur, London, Los Angeles, Mexico, New Delhi, New York, Paris, São Paulo, and Toronto; feature films may be found in Bangkok, Cologne, Jakarta, Seoul, Sydney, and Rome.

It appears that they initially built a core of canonical films from the post-war era. However, over the years they have been blessed by many smart staff members with broad tastes and complex notions of film history. The Japan Foundation has also been the repository for the subtitled prints of some of the original retrospectives in Japan and Europe, so their coverage is quite strong. The current shape of the collection reflects the tectonic shifts that have rocked the industry, as that older collection of studio masterpieces has been supplemented by an excellent selection of independent films from the last couple decades. It is safe to say that they have anywhere from one to ten films for all the major and minor contemporary directors. We also admire them for acquiring many historically important documentaries, most of which are deeply critical of the government.

There is a hitch. They will not show you their catalogue, an unfortunate policy that makes browsing for inspiration's sake impossible. Instead, users must submit a list of the films they are interested in showing, usually to the local Japan Foundation office, and their swift response will tell you whether they have the film. If they have it, they'll tell you the format, print condition, and the owner of the copyright. You arrange a rental payment with the distributor or studio, and the Foundation will send you the print for the cost of return shipping. It takes time, but it works.

Of course, there are some intransigent studios, notably Tōhō, who don't respond well to requests from what they think are minor customers. The attitude of other studios seems to change day-by-day, and some have recently been raising their rates to unreasonable levels. Independent filmmakers and distributors are easier, if the rights situation is clear. Sometimes it can be maddening. However, at least the Japan Foundation has an excellent collection representing most eras of Japanese cinema, and they are happy to lend prints if the copyright permissions are secured. It is a precious resource to festivals and universities around the world.

Note they also have grants for public events, as well as research grants for study in Japan.

The Rest

Here are a few other North American distributors of note:

Canyon Cinema
145 Ninth Street, Suite 260
San Francisco, CA 94103 U.S.A.
Phone/Fax: 415-626-2255
Website: www.canyoncinema.com

Criterion Pictures USA, Inc.
8238-40 Lehigh
Morton Grove, IL 60053-2615 U.S.A.
Phone: 847-470-8164
Toll Free: 800-890-9494
Fax: 847-470-8194
Website: www.criterionpicusa.com

The Film-Makers' Cooperative
c/o The Clocktower Gallery
108 Leonard Street, 13 floor
New York, NY 10013 U.S.A.
Phone: 212-267-5665
Fax: 212-267-5666
e-mail: film6000@aol.com
Website: www.film-makerscoop.com

Icarus
32 Court St., 21st Floor
Brooklyn, NY 11201 U.S.A.
Phone: 718-488-8900
Fax: 718-488-8642
email: mail@IcarusFilms.com
Website: www.icarusfilms.com

Janus Films
c/o Criterion Pictures USA, Inc.
email: booking@janusfilms.com

Kino International Corp.
333 W. 39th St., Ste. 503
New York, NY 10018 U.S.A.
Phone: 212-629-6880
Toll free: 800-562-3330

Fax: 212-714-0871
email: contact@kino.com
Website: www.kino.com

Milestone Films
P.O. Box 128
Harrington Park, New Jersey 07640-0128 U.S.A.
Phone: 800-603-1104
Fax: 201-767-3035
email: milefilms@gmail.com
Website: www.milestonefilms.com

MoMA Non-Theatrical Rentals
11 West 53 Street,
New York, NY 10019-5497 U.S.A.
Phone: 212-489-0299
Website: www.moma.org

Swank Motion Pictures
10795 Watson Road
St. Louis, MO 63127-1012 U.S.A.
Phone: 800-876-5577
Website: www.swank.com

III. Used Book and Video Stores

If you've got the book fetish, you must know about the following used bookstores (furuhon'ya). *We have listed only the stores with a preponderance of film books, journals and collectibles, the kind of shop that will likely have what you need and plenty of what you desire but can't afford. Although they are quickly disappearing in the hinterlands, most local used bookstores have a shelf of film books that are quite a bit cheaper than the specialty shops. It is always worth ducking in neighborhood stores, as treasures are surely waiting for you there.*

The Best

@Wonder

@ワンダー

@Wonder
2-5-4 Kanda Jinbōchō
Chiyoda-ku, Tokyo 101-0051 Japan
Tel/Fax: 03-3238-7415
email: wonder@atwonder.co.jp
Website: www.atwonder.co.jp/

Like Vintage, AtWonder focuses less on books than magazines and ephemera related to popular culture. This can include fields like sci-fi, sports, mystery stories, and subculture, but cinema is one of their strong points, with half of one of their two floors being dedicated to film. They have more ephemera than you can imagine: posters, pamphlets, handbills, stills, pressbooks, magazines (mostly centered on popular cinema), and other goodies, too. Their book section is also pretty good, with the entire back wall full of books that are usually priced cheaper than Isseidō and Yaguchi, and are not just concentrated in recent books.

Furuhon no Ogino

古本のオギノ

Furuhon no Ogino

1-13-20 Nipponbashi, Chūō-ku
Osaka 542-0073 Japan
Phone: 06-6631-2009

Directly across from the National Bunraku Theater, Furuhon no Ogino has a very good selection of books, programs, posters, and other unusual items. Now that Sugimoto Ryōkōdō has closed, perhaps temporarily, it is the best film bookshop in Kansai.

Kimoto Shoten
木本書店

Kimoto Shoten
6-86-15 Takinogawa, Kita-ku
Tokyo 114-0023
Phone: 03-3915-7018
Fax: 03-3916-8607
email: honya_kimoto@ybb.ne.jp

Kimoto is one of the older film-specialty *furuhon'ya* in Tokyo. The shop is small, but nearby they have both a *sōkō* (warehouse) and a branch store that fairly triples their size. The branch focusses more on popular items like manga, but the storage has a preponderance of film books and magazines. The upshot is that if you are looking for something specific it is worth asking the owner, even if it's not on the shelf.

Inagaki Shoten
稲垣書店

Inagaki Shoten
3-65-2 Arakawa, Arakawa-ku
Tokyo 116-0002
Phone: 03-3802-2828
Fax: 03-3807-7314

Inagaki is out of the way, but don't let that stand in the way of a visit. This is a small store with a big *sōkō*. The owner, Nakayama Shinnyo, is the most knowledgable of *furuhon'ya-san* and also the friendliest. He has even written a number of curious books about film *furuyon'ya* (for example *Furuhon'ya oyaji* [Tokyo: Chikuma Shobō, 2002]). You might get a cold shoulder from Yaguchi or feel corporate coldness from Isseidō, but a pleasant conversation with Nakayama-san is to be had at Inagaki. This is a particularly good store for tracking down core books and journals for Japanese film studies, no matter the time period. Call before you go because Nakayama-san has been concentrating on book fairs as of late, leaving the shop closed.

Isseidō Shoten
一誠堂書店

Isseidō Shoten
1-7 Kanda Jinbōchō
Chiyoda-ku, Tokyo 101-0051
Phone: 03-3292-0071
Fax: 03-3292-0095
email: mail@isseido-books.co.jp
Website: www.isseido-books.co.jp/

Founded in 1903, Isseidō is arguably the best and most professional of the used bookstores in Kanda that deal with film. They also cover a wide range of other fields, but they put considerable effort into cinema and publish a sizeable annual catalog (*mokuroku*) of what they have in stock. While the section for film books in the store—right at the entrance!—does not seem large at first, they have a considerable stock in their back rooms (especially of magazines). You can check that through their catalog; better yet, contact them directly and ask if they have what you need.

The store is tidy and well-organized, the staff attentive, and the organization is very experienced at dealing with foreign libraries. If you are trying to build up your university library, Isseidō is one of the first dealers you should contact to get out of print film books and runs of old film magazines. Indeed, along with Yaguchi they are one of the few places where you can find many of the core reference books we have identified as "The Best." They are one of the few dealers that will purchase used reprint series and rare books, such as early publications or vanity press imprints, so many sellers choose them. With that respect, they always have a good selection of books for sale. It's also, believe it or not, a good place to buy newly released books at a slight discount, as many comps seem to wind up on their shelves in the first few months of a book's life. If they don't have what you want, you can place a standing order and they will contact you if they find it.

The main problem with Isseidō is that they are so business-like, they also tend on average to be the most expensive of the used film bookstores. They rarely price books unreasonably above the market rate, but they also don't have many bargains. The best advice is to do some comparison shopping and check out some of the other Kanda bookstores first before going into Isseidō.

Vintage

Vintage
Jinbōchō Center Building 1F, 2F
2-5 Kanda Jinbōchō
Chiyoda-ku, Tokyo 101-0051 Japan
Phone/Fax:03-3261-3577
email: spvy7sn9@gamma.ocn.ne.jp
Website: www17.ocn.ne.jp/~vintage

Vintage features a massive offering of ephemera for film, television and music. They stock popular post-war magazines and a smattering of older books and journals, but the main attractions are the posters, pamphlets, theater programs, still photographs, press packs and tickets. Prices are fine-tuned to fandom desires, and thus span a very wide range.

Yaguchi Shoten
矢口書店

Yaguchi Shoten
2-5-1 Kanda Jinbōchō
Chiyoda-ku, Tokyo 101-0051 Japan
Phone: 03-3261-5708
Fax: 03-3261-6350
email: yaguchi@mbk.nifty.com
Website: homepage3.nifty.com/yaguchi

Established in 1918, Yaguchi is the oldest used bookstore specializing in cinema and theater. Their selection tends not to be as deep as Isseidō's, but chances are good that they will have a lot that interests you, whether it be books, journals, screenplays, old magazines, pamphlets, handbills, and the like. It used to have a reputation for occasionally unreasonable pricing, but it has gotten better in recent years and tends, on average, to be a little cheaper than Isseidō. They are a smaller and less business-like operation than Isseidō, but they have tried to start dealing with foreign libraries and publish a sizeable catalog, so they are another store to contact to build up your library. Their homepage has a helpful online database, but the store itself is a fun place to browse. It's just down the street from Isseidō, so make sure to check out both before buying.

The Rest

Abe no Sutanpu Koin
アベノスタンプコイン

Abe no Sutanpu Koin
Kanda Kosho Sentā Biru 6F
2-3 Kanda Jinbōchō
Chiyoda-ku, Tokyo 101-0051 Japan
Phone: 03-3264-2566

Abe no Sutanpu Koin is a messy shop on an upper floor of the Kanda Kosho Center, which contains many other stores of interest. There are a few bookshelves with old magazines and books. The real riches, however, are piled high in cardboard boxes. There are thousands upon thousands of stills, programs, and posters to rummage through. Nothing is in order. But you never know. They also cater to a few other manias, from sumo to trains. It's a wonderful spot to pick up some cheap and charming *omiyage,* although we note a marked crescendo in the chaos so do not be surprised if it disappears overnight.

Bunken Rokku Saido
ブンケン・ロック・サイド

Bunken Rokku Saido
2-3 Kanda-Jinbōchō
Chiyoda-ku, Tokyo 101-0051 Japan
Phone/Fax: 03-3511-8227
Website: homepage2.nifty.com/bunken

Like its sister shop Bunken Shoin, Bunken Rokku Saido focuses on subculture, especially idols and rock n' roll. But they are building up their collection of film-related materials, especially magazines and pamphlets, and are thus worth a look even if they do not have the volume of AtWonder and Vintage, which are just down the street.

Culture Station
カルチャーステーション

Culture Station
3-32-23 Hachimanyama
Setagaya-ku, Tokyo 156-0056 Japan

Phone/Fax: 03-5317-4901
Website: www.culturestation.co.jp

This is where you can pick up your original Hirose Ryōko tea pot, along with beer posters, jigsaw puzzles and just about anything else emblazoned with your favorite idol's mug. Most of their shelf space is devoted to popular magazines. The back walls are even organized by idol, so special issues concerning a given personality are concentrated in one spot. This is all about mania, so don't expect anything terribly old . . . or about male *tarento* for that matter. Culture Station is conveniently located just down the road from Ōya Sōichi, so on the way back to the station you can pick up the original of something you saw at the library.

Kamakura Kinema-dō
鎌倉キネマ堂

Kamakura Kinema-dō
Daiichi Ōtani Building
2-11-11 Komachi
Kamakura-shi, Kanagawa 248-0006 Japan
Phone/Fax: 0467-22-6667
email: kinemado@kamakuranet.ne.jp
Website: www.kinemado.com

The proprietor of this establishment, who worked for a long time in the record industry, was an enthusiastic film fan who collected enough books that he started selling them over the net. When that was not enough, he opened up a small café that also serves as a bookstore and screening site. Located at the end of a narrow alley by the Hato Sabure store on Wakamiya Ōdori, it is full of books, posters, and the music of Ishihara Yūjirō, but not many seats. You can still order books through the website, but if you are visiting Kamakura, perhaps to visit the graves of Ozu and Kinoshita in Engakuji, this is worth a brief stop, if only for a cup of tea.

Marubell-dō
マルベル堂

Maruberu-dō Shin Nakamise-ten
Shin Nakamise Arcade
1-30-6 Asakura
Taitō-ku, Tokyo 111-0032 Japan
Phone/Fax: 03-3844-1445
email: sinnaka@marubell.co.jp

Website: www.marubell.co.jp/promaide/promaido.html

Seeing as we are introducing a few places that don't really sell books, we have to mention Marubell, the 80-year-old-plus dealer in bromides (sometimes "promides"). Bromides are basically pocket-sized star photos or stills sold to fans (Aaron's mother-in-law has a whole stack of them from the 1950s). Japan used to have *buromaido-ya* all over the place, but Marubell, which was one of the first, is now one of the last. Located near Sensōji in Asakusa, it sells images of everyone from old-time movie stars to new idols to prowrestlers—but not too cheap (it's about ¥300-400 for a small photo). If you're visiting Asakusa, make sure to walk through Rokku (the old movie theater district) and look for the remains of the Denkikan and the Taishōkan, go to Sensōji and find the Eiga Benshizuka (a memorial for *benshi*), and then drop by Marubell to get a snapshot of your silver screen love.

There are also a few websites that represent coalitions of used bookstores. They have none of the sublime pleasures or potential surprises of a storefront stuffed to the gills with musty old books, but they're certainly useful in a pinch.

Jimbou
じんぼう

Website: jimbou.info

This is the official website for the booksellers in Jinbōchō, one of the highest concentration of used bookstores in the world. The website has a searchable database, news on fairs and other events, and a slick interactive map of the area.

Nihon no Furuhon'ya
日本の古本屋

Website: www.kosho.or.jp

This is probably the easiest way to track down a used book. Their network stretches the breadth of Japan. The problem is that if you do not live in Japan, someone else will have to pay for the book (unless you have a Japanese bank with online services). Many booksellers are also unwilling to ship internationally.

Finally, here are some other good used bookstores. Most are online shops with no storefronts.

Cinebeam
『シネビーム』
Website: cineb.net

ebiya books
『えびや・フックス』
Website: www.ebiya-books.com

Furuhon Hibaridō
『古本ひばり堂』
Website: hibari.ocnk.net

Furuhon'ya 451
『古本屋451』
Website: homepage2.nifty.com/huruhonya451

Machiyadō
『町屋堂』
Website: www.fiberbit.net/user/machiya-do

Moviebox
『ムービーボックス』
Website: www2.comco.ne.jp/~libro

Tanabe Shoten
『たなべ書店』
Website: www.tanabeshoten.co.jp

If you are reading this chapter, then you must have the bug, just like us. You know the keen pleasures of an afternoon ramble from bookstore to bookstore (what we call furuhon'ya burabura*). The next three entries are suggestions for just such an occasion.*

Furuhon'ya burabura: Chūō Line

Many literary figures and filmmakers in the postwar era have lived near stations on the JR Chūō Line. We suspect this is because it is the most convenient train for late-night romps in Shinjuku, for a long time the most important social space for those in the arts. This may help explain why the bookstores on the Chūō Line are also prime spots for anyone who loves film books. Both of us have lived on this line, and our shelves are lined with books we bumped into in places like Ogikubo, Kōenji and Kichijōji. Find one store, and they'll supply a map for all the others.

Furuhon'ya burabura: Minami-Morimachi to Tenma

While the number of bookstores in this neighborhood of Osaka is nothing like the concentration in Takadanobaba or the Tokyo Chūō Line, there are enough shops here to make it worth a visit. Most of the *furuhon'ya* are in the covered arcade between Minami-Morimachi subway station and JR Tenma Station.

Furuhon'ya burabura: Waseda to Takadanobaba

Website: www.w-furuhon.net

There are over two dozen used bookstores between the Tōzai Line's Waseda Station and JR Takadanobaba Station. Many have film books and magazines, and the prices are far lower than Jinbōchō. From Waseda pass the Hachimangu Shrine and head down Waseda-dōri; from Takadanobaba, turn right from the JR station and the bookstores start after you cross Meiji-dōri; from Nishiwaseda, head north on Meiji-dōri and turn right on Waseda-dōri. Their website has a map. Of special note is Bunshōdō, which has thousands of stills, posters, lobby cards, pressbooks and other emphemera, and Bun'eidō, which probably has the best selection of film books and magazines.

IV. Annotated Bibliography for Bibliographic Studies

Bunkenshi / Bibliographic Studies

This section includes the curious stream of historiographic investigation dominated by a handful of collectors-cum-scholars. These are men with the collecting bug, crazy fellows who directed their fetishistic energies toward text rather than film prints and bromides. We benefit greatly from their love of words over stars and celluloid, as they published handy books that map out the discursive terrain of Japanese film history.

These works are useful not only for the attempts they represent to create a history of film-related publishing, but also often in considering the science of how to categorize film knowledge. This has practical implications. One may want to research industrial trends in the 1950s, for instance, but since most Japanese systems only classify film books under broad categories such as "cinema" (eiga) *or "cinema history"* (eigashi) *with few specific sub-categories, one is forced to plow through a bunch of texts until an appropriate one is found. While some institutions like the National Museum of Modern Art, Tokyo, the National Film Center (23-25), have endeavored to formulate in-house classification systems that better accommodate the range of film publications than the National Diet Library Classification, these are not generally available. Since the inadequacy of categorization in some ways parallels the lack of attention given to film by intellectual society, the attempts by these individual authors to arrange the wealth of film knowledge is also an often desperate attempt to solidify film studies as a respectable discipline. The systems they create can be odd at times, but on a practical level they can still serve as catalogs that can help you determine what books have been written on a particular subject.*

We list them in chronological order of the years covered.

Nihon eiga shoshi, by Yamaguchi Takemi
Tokyo: Eiga Hyōronsha, 1937.
山口竹美著『日本映画書誌』映画評論社, 1937.

The first major reference book for film publications, covering 1897-1937 and organized by year. Yamaguchi provides extensive bibliographic data. This includes tables of contents and page ranges, which would be convenient for ordering through interlibrary loan. The back of the book includes a year-by-year list of film periodicals' inaugural issues, although it is incomplete and lacks date ranges. Yamaguchi's own corrections are appended to the reprint in *Kindai eiga engeki ongaku shoshi,* ed. Makino Mamoru (Tokyo: Yumani Shobō, 1992) (see below).

Eiga bunkenshi, by Okada Shinkichi
Tokyo: Dai Nihon Eiga Kyōkai, 1943.
岡田真吉著『映画文献史』大日本映画協会, 1943.

One of the few memorable books from the wartime Nihon eiga sensho series produced by the Dai Nihon Eiga Kyōkai, Okada Shinkichi's work provides a narrative history of film books (followed by translations of pieces by six of his favorite French silent film theorists). Considering it was published at the height of "Greater East Asian War," its focus on European and American books and concomitant exclusion of Japanese writers is utterly mysterious. Okada is self-conscious about the present state of total war. He assures readers he took great care when writing about enemies (which might explain the apparently structured absence of Eisenstein). He also takes great pride in the fact that, with access to foreign books off limits, his book lets people know what they're missing! Needless to say, this makes it mostly useful as a map of what foreign film books were circulating in pre-war/wartime Japan.

Kindai eiga engeki ongaku shoshi, edited by Makino Mamoru
Tokyo: Yumani Shobō, 1992.
牧野守編集・解題『近代映画・演劇・音楽書誌』ゆまに書房, 1992.

An eight-volume reprint of prewar bibliographies and periodical indexes. The first volume reprints Yamaguchi Takemi's *Nihon eiga shoshi* (see above). In there, books are arranged by publication date with a title and author index and tables of contents for most entries. Volumes two through five reprint the index of articles and books on cinema and the performing arts published monthly by Takarazuka's library. It covers the years 1936 to 1944, and while the subject classification is still broad—and you have to look at each month's issue to follow a subject—entries list page numbers (unlike Makino's *Nihon eiga bunken shoshi* [p. 81]) and can thus help with interlibrary loan. The last two volumes of this Yumani reprint feature a fantastic collection of articles on *bunkenshi* selected by Makino Mamoru. The earliest is from 1910, the latest from 1943. The articles are a grab bag: thematic lists, book reviews, historical narratives, and the entirety of Okada Shinkichi's 1943 *Eiga bunkenshi* (see above). The *bekkan* contains Makino's own history of Japanese film bibliography, as well as supplemental reprints on film journalism, film bibliography, and statistics.

Nihon eiga bunkenshi, by Imamura Miyoo
Tokyo: Kagamiura Shobō, 1967.
今村三四夫著『日本映画文献史』鏡浦書房, 1967.

Although displaced from its position of authority by Tsuji Kyōhei's *Jiten eiga no tosho* and marred by mistakes, *Nihon eiga bunkenshi* remains an essential reference work for Japanese film. Imamura published it as a response to Okada's emphasis on foreign works and their translations. He splits his book into three parts—books, periodicals, newsletters—each beginning with a general history of film publishing. The first lists about 1,200 books with their tables of contents. The second gives extremely valuable abstracts explaining the nature of each periodical and its key authors; this is now what makes the book indispensable. He finishes up with short sections on fliers, posters, and a history of film criticism in daily newspapers. Imamura's bibliography includes historical accounts of the development of film publishing. This makes it especially useful for starting research on the history of film journalism or film studies.

Jiten eiga no tosho, by Tsuji Kyōhei
Tokyo: Gaifūsha, 1989.
辻恭平著『事典　映画の図書』凱風社, 1989.

We *love* this book. It is unquestionably the most important bibliography in Japanese film studies. Everyone should get one, but it will set you back a small bundle at this point. Tsuji researched this book by travelling around Japan, visiting libraries to see if they had any unknown jewels. He came across quite a few and diligently notes which library holds these unique items. Combined with his considerable personal collection and the advice of his scholarly and collector friends, he amassed a wealth of data on ninety years of film publishing history. The book's indexes list 4,863 books by 3,170 authors; add the journals and newsletters and it all adds up to nearly 6,000 entries. Each of these supplements the usual bibliographic data with notes on contents. The subject headings may still be too broad, but Tsuji makes an effort to group books within these larger headings by specific subjects (e.g., director name). It's *the* first and foremost resource for Japanese film studies, hands down.

Katte ni eigasho kō, by Shigemasa Takafumi
Osaka: Matsumoto Kōbō, 1997.
重政隆文著『勝手に映画書・考』松本工房, 1997.
Eiga no hon no hon, by Shigemasa Takafumi
Osaka: Matsumoto Kōbō, 2002.
重政隆文著『映画の本の本』松本工房, 2002.

Eiga hihyō wa hihyō dekiru ka. Bangaihen, by Shigemasa Takafumi
Osaka: Matsumoto Kōbō, 2003.
重政隆文著『映画批評は批評できるか　番外編』松本工房, 2003.

A series of three books attempting to review literally hundreds of books on film. Given that this was done by one individual, a professor at Osaka University of Arts, it is both a bit obsessive and inevitably personal, but it can offer a meta-perspective on film writing that is not easy to find. The third book focuses on publications by those who are not film critics or scholars.

Furuhon'ya "shinebukku" manpo, by Nakayama Shinnyo
Tokyo: Waizu Shuppan, 1999.
中山信如著『古本屋「シネブック」漫歩』ワイズ出版, 1999.

A charming personal account of film books and periodicals by the knowledgeable owner of Inagaki Shoten, a Tokyo used bookstore specializing in cinema (64-65). It covers about 800 books, organized by subject (e.g., "Books on Kawashima Yūzō"). It is a perspective quite different from Shigemasa Takafumi's, in part because it also notes not just the history but also the market rate of these books.

ARTICLES ON THE HISTORY OF FILM CRITICISM

Anderson, Joseph, "Japanese Film Periodicals," *The Quarterly of Film, Radio and Television* 9.4 (Summer 1955): 410-423.

Gonda Yasunosuke, "Honpō eiga shakai mondai kankeisho kaisetsu," *Ōhara shakai mondai kenkyūjo zasshi,* 1.3, 1.4, 1.5 (Sept.-Nov. 1934). (Also in *Kindai eiga engeki ongaku shoshi,* pp. 402-444.)

Iijima Tadashi, "Boku no hihyōshi," *Eiga hyōron* 15.6 (June 1958).

Iwamoto Kenji, "Film Criticism and the Study of Cinema in Japan: A Historical Survey," *Iconics* (1987): 129-146.

"*Kinema junpō* sōkan 1,000-gō eiga nisshi," *Kinema junpō* 185 (September Tokubetsugō, 1957): 165-186.

Kishi Matsuo, "Nengetsu to eiga hihyō: Garyū honpō eiga hihyōka shi 1-14," *Eiga hyōron* 21.10-22.2, 22.6-23.2 (September 1964-December 1965).

Makino Mamoru, "Nihon eiga zasshi hensenshi 1," *Kinema junpō* 1135 (July 1, 1994): 26-31; and Makino Mamoru, "Nihon eiga zasshi hensenshi 2," *Kinema junpō* 1137 (July 15, 1994): 40-45; also see adjacent articles.

Togawa Naoki, et al., "Nihon eiga hihyō hattatsushi 1-10," *Kinema junpō* 1191-1194, 1195, 1197-2002 (May 1-October 1, 1996).

Wada Norie, "Nihon eiga ronsōshi," *Kinema junpō* 156 (July 1957).

Yoshiyama Kyokkō, *Nihon eigakai jibutsu kigen* (Tokyo: "Shinema to Engei" Sha, 1933), 170-181.

Anthologies of Film Criticism and Kōza

There are literally hundreds of books of film criticism or theory published by individual authors or as anthologies. Only a few, however, have attempted to collect a broad range of film writings from a historical perspective, or to bring together the best criticism or scholarship of the time in multi-volume works. Such works not only provide informative pieces on various topics but also serve to define the direction, scope, nature and depth of film studies or film culture. Since many are collections of magazine articles, they can also help if your library—like most outside of Japan—doesn't have many Japanese film journals.

Besuto obu Kinema junpō, 1950-1993
Tokyo: Kinema Junpōsha, 1994.
『ベスト・オブ・キネマ旬報 = The best of Kinema junpo』キネマ旬報社, 1994.

These two thick volumes assemble some of the most important articles to appear in *Kinema junpō* since 1950. This can be very useful for foreign scholars since few institutions have *Kinema junpō* this far back, despite the fact it is Japan's most important film magazine. Because they reproduce the *KineJun* pages as is, they even throw in a few movie ads.

Eiga e no omoi: Nihon eigashi tanbō, edited by Eigashi Kenkyūshi Kankō Iinkai
Nitta-chō: Tanaka Jun'ichirō Kinen Nihon Eigashi Fesutibaru Jikkō Iinkai, 1998-2003.
映画史研究誌刊行委員会編集『映画への思い 日本映画史探訪』田中純一郎記念日本映画史フェスティバル実行委員会, 1998-2003.

This is less an anthology or a *kōza* than a set of six catalogs centered on film history, each published yearly in conjunction with a film history festival sponsored by Nitta in honor of its former resident, Tanaka Jun'ichirō. As a whole, the catalogs feature not just writings on or by Tanaka, but also reprints of some of the rare historical documents in his collection and original pieces of scholarship by new researchers. They also contain a complete bibliography of Tanaka's writings.

Eiga hyōron no jidai, edited by Satō Tadao and Kishikawa Shin
Tokyo: Katarogu Hausu, 2003.
佐藤忠男, 岸川真編著『「映画 評論」の時代 = The Film crit, the Eiga hyoron, the magazine of film review, movie critique and underground』カタログハウス, 2003.

A one-volume collection of articles from *Eiga hyōron*, one of *KineJun's* main competitors. Not as extensive a collection as *Besuto obu Kinema junpō* (above), but it does still include a table of contents for the magazine after 1950.

Eigaron kōza, edited by Yamada Kazuo
Tokyo: Gōdō Shuppan, 1977-1978.
山田和夫編集『映画論講座』合同出版, 1977-1978.

A four-volume collection mostly penned by writers and filmmakers associated with the Japanese Communist Party. The volumes cover, in order: film theory, film history, filmmaking, and film movements.

Filme aus Japan
Berlin: Freunde der Deutschen Kinemathek, 1993.

Filme aus Japan is a compendium of German-language criticism on Japanese cinema, starting with a 1924 essay on Sessue Hayakawa by Béla Balász and ending with a 1965 translation of Richie. There are 56 articles in all, followed by 48 short biographies, and 102 film synopses that quote various books and articles in several languages. There are also important essays (all in German) by Itami Mansaku, Masumura Yasuzō, Ōshima Nagisa and others.

Gendai eiga kōza, edited by Wada Norie
Tokyo: Sōgensha, 1954-1955.
和田矩衞編『現代映画講座』創元社, 1954-1955.

An interesting slice of thinking on film in the mid-1950s. The six volumes cover, in order: production and history, technology, screenwriting, directing, acting, and film appreciation.

Gendai Nihon eigaron taikei, edited by Ogawa Tōru
Tokyo: Tōjusha, 1970-1972.
『現代日本映画論大系』冬樹社, 1970-1972.

One of the most important postwar publications on film, this 6-volume work is a collection of postwar film criticism arranged by era (about 4 years per volume) and subject. The selection reflects the biases of the editors, but as a whole it is a superb cross-section of film debates and film discourse over 25 years. Each volume also contains commentaries and bibliographies of the other major articles published during the period that were not included in the anthology.

Imamura Taihei eizō hyōron
Tokyo: Yumani Shobō, 1991.
『今村太平映像評論』ゆまに書房, 1991.

Reprints of ten of the prewar and wartime books of Imamura Taihei, one of Japan's most important film critics and theorists, famous especially for his writings on documentary, realism, visual culture, and animation. These are particularly valuable because they are facsimilies of the relatively rare first editions. Imamura, like many writers often revised his postwar editions, sometimes substantively.

Kōza Nihon eiga, edited by Imamura Shōhei, et al.
Tokyo: Iwanami Shoten, 1985-1988.
今村昌平他編集『講座　日本映画』岩波書店, 1985-1988.

The best multi-volume anthology (*kōza*) on Japanese cinema so far. In eight volumes divided by historical period, it is full of interviews of historically important film professionals and original articles by top scholars. Each volume contains serialized articles by Satō Tadao and Shindō Kaneto on Japanese film history and the history of screenwriting respectively (the latter was collected into *Nihon shinario-shi* [Iwanami Shoten, 1989]).

Nihon eigaron gensetsu taikei, edited by Makino Mamoru
Tokyo: Yumani Shobō, 2003-2006.
牧野守監修『日本映画論言説大系』ゆまに書房, 2003-2006.

Thirty volumes worth of reprints (sometimes reprinting multiple books per volume) of some of the major works of prewar film theory and criticism, including some rare works that were never fully distributed in the first place. Lengthy and excellent commentaries (*kaisetsu*) can be found in each volume. Features work by major figures like Gonda Yasunosuke, Iwasaki Akira, Tsumura Hideo, Iijima Tadashi, Kaeriyama Norimasa, Shimizu Hikaru, Hasegawa Nyozekan, Itagaki Takao, Kitagawa Fuyuhiko, Kishi Matsuo, and Yanai Yoshio, as well as reprints of the Diet debates on the Film Law.

Nihon eigashi sōsho, edited by Iwamoto Kenji, et al.
Tokyo: Shinwasha, 2004-.
岩本憲児他編集『日本映画史叢書』森話社, 2004-.

A multi-volume series (still in production) featuring tomes on Japanese film and nationalism, gender, WWII, the 1960s, *jidaigeki,* melodrama, and other topics. Many of the books are edited by Iwamoto Kenji and notably feature research by some of today's younger film scholars.

Puroretaria eiga undō no tenbō, edited by Shinkō Eigasha
Tokyo: Taihōkaku Shobō, 1930.
新興映画社編『プロレタリア映画運動の展望』大鳳閣書房, 1930.
Reprinted online by UM Center for Japanese Studies Publications Program: hdl.handle.net/2027/spo.bbx2327.0001.001

This is a reader edited by "Shinkō Eigasha"—a film collective, not a company. The title page lists 20 authors, including high profile names from the proletarian literature and film scene like Iwasaki Akira, Kishi Matsuo, Kobayashi Takiji, and Kurahara Korehito. The articles were gathered from Prokino publications, and represent a self-portrait of the film movement at the height of its activity.

Saisentan minshū goraku eiga bunken shiryōshū, edited by Makino Mamoru
Tokyo: Yumani Shobō, 2006.
牧野守監修『最尖端民衆娯楽映画文献資料集』ゆまに書房, 2006.

Eighteen volumes long, this reprint series contains more popular-oriented books than Makino's *Nihon eigaron gensetsu taikei*, such as novelizations of *Zigomar*, star bios, censorship anecdotes, and books by important figures like Tanaka Eizō, Ushihara Kiyohiko, and Kaeriyama Norimasa.

And, finally, we would be remiss if we did not emphasize all the scholarly introductions accompanying the reprints of Japanese journals and books, particularly those edited by Makino Mamoru. Together, they constitute a rigorous and impressive history of prewar and wartime film theory and criticism in Japan.

Indexes and Bibliographies

Indexes and bibliographies are clearly the heart of bibliographic studies, but the emphasis of the works listed below is on indexing rather than studying, on listing rather than mapping.

The Best

Eiga, ongaku, geinō no hon zenjōhō 45/94
Tokyo: Nichigai Asoshiētsu, 1997.
『映画・音楽・芸能の本全情報 45/94』日外アソシエーツ, 1997.

Eiga, ongaku, geinō no hon zenjōhō 95/99
Tokyo: Nichigai Asoshiētsu, 2000.
『映画・音楽・芸能の本全情報 95/99』日外アソシエーツ, 2000.
Eiga, ongaku, geinō no hon zenjōhō 2000-2004
Tokyo: Nichigai Asoshiētsu, 2005.
『映画・音楽・芸能の本全情報 2000-2004』日外アソシエーツ, 2005.

This hardly belongs in the company below, if only because it's nearly impossible to use. However, one is hard pressed to find decent indexes of recent film books. These three volumes list film, music and entertainment books published in the postwar era. They appear fairly comprehensive, but are frustrating to use. The print is small and cramped. The top handful of critics and directors get their own sections, but all other categories are so broadly construed so as to be meaningless. And they are marred by embarrassing mistakes (incorrect characters for Hasumi Shigehiko of all people!?!). Thankfully, the tables of contents are included for most books by the third effort—thankfully, because there is little reason to use this for the period pre-dating *Jiten eiga no tosho* (74). Until another Imamura or Tsuji comes along, this at least takes care of the considerable chunk of time between 1989 and the present-day.

Kenji Mizoguchi, a Guide to References and Resources, by Paul Andrew and Dudley Andrew
Boston: G.K. Hall, 1981.

We have consciously left out books on individual filmmakers simply because they are the easiest items to find. A name search in WorldCat or Waseda University's online catalog will easily pull them up. Needless to say, there are many dozens of such books and in many languages. At the same time, we want to highlight one above all, and not simply because it's in English. Most bibliographies for filmmakers are simple lists, and the Japanese publications rarely include writings in foreign languages. By way of contrast, *Kenji Mizoguchi, a Guide to References and Resources* provides superb annotations for every entry. It starts with a critical survey of the director's career which remains one of the best essays on Mizoguchi, followed by a filmography with synopses. However, the meat of this thick book is the bibliography, which includes reviews, essays, interviews and books for Japanese, English, French and other languages. The annotations are lengthy, refreshingly analytical, contain extensive quotes, and actually make for pleasurable reading. One can learn a lot about Mizoguchi Kenji just by reading this bibliography. The Andrew brothers' book is a model for all of us to strive for—indeed, it was one of ours for the book in your hand.

Kinema junpō February 15 issues

Starting in the mid-1970s, the venerable film magazine *Kinema junpō* started producing an annual special issue that sums up the previous year in film. These are popularly known for their "Best of…" surveys, which are trivial, unscientific affairs. However, the rest of the numbers are packed with vital information, starting with a full index of the previous volume. They also include data on the state of the film and video industries, a list of festival award winners, the slates of domestic film festivals, a list of books published, and various articles summarizing the year's events, problems, and controversies. One of the most important sections is their chart of all films released that year, listed by studio and release date; this chart includes cast and credits, running time, and issue numbers for *Kinema junpō* articles. In the prewar era, *Kinema junpō's* January or February issues include a "Reference Chart of New Pictures." It generally lists only foreign works, and provides information about each film's distributor and studio, sound vs. silent, number of reels, stars, and the issue number for its critical review. Note that the Waseda Tsubouchi Memorial Theatre Museum keeps the last three decades of indexes collected in a single binder. In the 1930s, *KineJun* also published a similar issue every January 1.

Nihon eiga bunken shoshi: Meiji, Taishōki, by Makino Mamoru
Tokyo: Yūshōdō, 2003.
牧野守編『日本映画文献書誌: 明治・大正期』雄松堂, 2003.

The product of decades of indefatigable effort by Makino Mamoru, one of the titans of *bunkenshi,* to personally index every issue of every prewar film magazine. He diligently includes coterie publications. This index is extremely valuable because nothing else exists of its kind and scale. It still can be hard to use, however, as it is only arranged by year and article title, without subject headings. The author and film title index can make it easier to research individual authors or films, but not broader subjects. Makino has also prepared an early Shōwa version, but it remains on a variety of media—everything from *wapuro* to handwritten recipe cards. A CD-ROM version is desperately needed, but it, like the early Shōwa volume, is not likely to appear anytime soon.

Ōya Sōichi Bunko zasshi kiji sakuin sōmokuroku: Jinmei hen, kenmei hen.
Tokyo: Ōya Sōichi Bunko: Sōhatsubaimoto Kinokuniya Shoten, 1985.
『大宅壮一文庫雑誌記事索引総目録. 人名編. 件名編.』大宅壮一文庫, 1985.

This is the primary printed index to popular periodicals prepared by the Ōya Sōichi Library and covers the period from the Meiji era to 1985. Later printed supplements extend the index to 1995. After that, the web version (154), which only introduces works after 1988, is the primary resource. The index is basically divided into two parts: a name index, which offers a wealth of resources especially for star studies, and a subject index, one that is sufficiently detailed that there are headings for individual films, genres, studios, profession, etc. The index does not in general include film magazines, and can be spotty the farther back you go, but the coverage of postwar popular magazines is exceptional.

The Rest

An Annotated Bibliography for Chinese Film Studies, by Jim Cheng
Hong Kong: Hong Kong University Press, 2004.

This excellent bibliography has a fine section on the Manchurian Motion Picture Association, and various entries from the era when Japan tried to make Chinese cinema Japanese.

Chihō eigasho shishi: Hokkaidō, Tōhoku chihō, by Fujikawa Chisui
Kumamoto: Chisui Bunko, 1988.
藤川治水著『地方映画書私誌』治水文庫, 1988.

A self-published bibliography of local film histories (see pp. 142-144), focusing on northern Japan. Fujikawa was one of the leading proponents of local film historiography.

Eiga no naka no hon'ya to toshokan, by Iijima Tomoko
Tokyo: Nihon Tosho Kankōkai, 2004-2006.
飯島朋子著『映画の中の本屋と図書館』日本図書館刊行会, 2004-2006.

We could not resist including this two-volume reference book, a strange and wonderful filmography and bibliography about film and libraries. Written by a librarian (most likely for librarians), it is your front door to research on the cinematic representation of libraries in world cinema.

Eiga zasshi sōkangō mokuroku, by Tsukada Yoshinobu
Tokyo: Tsukada Yoshinobu (private printing), 1965-1985.
塚田嘉信著『映画雑誌創刊号目録』塚田嘉信(私版), 1965-1985.

This is a famous labor of love by Tsukada Yoshinobu that lists information about the initial issues of every film magazine he could find, from Taishō 2 (1913) to the mid-1980s (671 in all). As one might imagine, the fact that it lists only the contents of the first issues limits its usefulness. The other problem is that less than 50 copies of each volume were published, and the only libraries that seem to have it are Waseda and the Film Center. (It has been seen on the used book market, but you would certainly drop a mighty sum to pick it up.) Tsukada and others self-published a number of other books that list magazine indexes, but the proliferation of reprints in the last couple decades has made them largely irrelevant.

Ichikawa Kon: A Guide to References and Resources, by John Allyn
Boston: G.K. Hall, 1985.

The author first came into contact with Japanese film as a soldier, when he served as liaison between the Occupation and the motion picture industry. A companion to the Mizoguchi reference guide (80), Allyn attempts to collect all references to Ichikawa in Japanese, English and French. After a brief biography and critical survey, the bulk of the book is taken up by a filmography (1946-1980) with credits, data and fairly lengthy synopses. The next section is an excellent annotated bibliography of writings about and by Ichikawa (ranging from 1956 to 1979). There are just a handful of Japanese-language sources and the listing of archival sources is surely out of date. However, for researching English and French writings on the first half of Ichikawa's long career, this remains a vital resource.

Nihon eiga zasshi taitoru sōran, by Honchi Haruhiko
Tokyo: Waizu Shuppan, 2003.
本地陽彦編著『日本映画雑誌タイトル総覧』ワイズ出版, 2003.

This book lists 1,100 first issues of film magazines from the beginning up to 2000 by the year each started publication. While it is currently in print and easy to find, it is no substitute for Tsukada's *Eiga zasshi sōkangō mokuroku*. It is mainly fun to browse through the 80 pages of magazine covers.

"Purokino kanren bunken risuto," by Makino Mamoru
Gendai to shisō 19 (March 1975): 113-117.
牧野守著「プロキノ関連文献リスト」『現代と思想』(1975年3月):113-117.

Makino Mamoru appended this short, but excellent, bibliography of writings about and by the Proletarian Film League of Japan to a roundtable he conducted with former members of the movement. It lists many items that would easily escape the notice of researchers.

Shōwa shoki sayoku eiga zasshi bekkan
Tokyo: Senki Fukkokuban Kankōkai, 1981.
『昭和初期左翼映画雑誌別巻』戦旗復刻版刊行会, 1981.

In 1981, former members of Prokino produced a fine reprint of the left-wing film movement's journals and newspapers. This, the *bekkan* to that, contains an issue-by-issue table of contents for *Shinkō eiga*, *Prokino*, *Puroretaria eiga*, and *Eiga kurabu*. It also indexes the magazines by author. This material is prefaced by a series of reminiscences by former members and a *kaisetsu* for the reprint.

Takarazuka Bungei Toshokan geppō
『宝塚文芸図書館月報』

Takarazuka Bungei Toshokan geppō ran from 1936 to 1944 and is reprinted in Makino Mamoru's *Kindai eiga engeki ongaku shoshi* (73). This monthly publication indexed a wide variety of magazines, and noted the new books acquired by the library. The second volume has a year-long series on film. The index covers notable articles from a given month's magazines; most of the major magazines and many minor ones are covered. The section on film is divided into a number of sub-headings, such as scenarios, film management, theory, and the like, which are helpful but not that analytical. The index is by no means complete, but it often gives page numbers for articles, which can help a lot with interlibrary loan. On the other hand, each section includes articles from performing arts journals that film scholars rarely crack. Someone working on this period would certainly do well to troll through each issue, as unusual references would surely pop up.

Film Yearbooks and Almanacs

Film yearbooks are essential for understanding the state of cinema in any one year. They are startlingly rich sources of information. Most provide a detailed synchronic depiction of the industry, providing statistics (on production, distribution, exhibition/box office, imports and exports, censorship, etc.), the make-up of various companies, theaters and institutions, accounts of the year's events, and lists of films and personnel. In some cases, film critics have a greater hand and turn the yearbook, either whole or in part, into a critical account of the state of film art, partially by providing introductions or critiques of the films produced that year. Yearbooks, then, are often the first place to look when researching a period or an aspect of the industry.

The earliest yearbooks have been reprinted, as have unpublished manuscripts for yearbooks from the final years of the war. There were even English yearbooks between 1936 and 1939. Nearly every year since 1925 is represented by at least one publication; however, there have been a wide array of publishers and approaches over the years, so your first stop should be Section 031 of Tsuji's Jiten eiga no tosho (74). *We only include the longer-lasting and/or interesting ones here.*

The Best

Eiga nenkan
Tokyo: Jiji Eiga Tsūshinsha.
『映画年鑑』時事映画通信社.

The primary and longest running film yearbook. Jiji Tsūshinsha published the first postwar version from 1950 to 1970, then Jiji Eiga Tsūshinsha took over from 1973. Good for statistics, industry make-up, filmographies, as well as for articles about events each year. There are business reports by each company and film-related institution (such as Eirin or Eiren) and lists of their personnel. You can even get the home address of many film people. Each volume has a separate guide, *Eigakan meibo,* listing all the film theaters in the country.

Eiga nenkan. Shōwa hen I, edited by Kokusai Eiga Tsūshinsha
Tokyo: Nihon Tosho Sentā, 1994.
国際映画通信社編集『映画年鑑　昭和編 I』日本図書センター, 1994.
Eiga nenkan. Sengo hen, edited by Iwamoto Kenji and Makino Mamoru
Tokyo: Nihon Tosho Sentā, 1998.
岩本憲児, 牧野守監修『映画年鑑　戦後編』日本図書センター, 1998.

These two are very important reprints of nearly 30 years of film yearbooks produced under different titles. The *Shōwa hen* covers 1926 through 1945 with *nenkan* from Kokusai Eiga Tsūshinsha, and the *Sengo hen* includes annual issues from Jiji Tsūshinsha between 1950 and 1960. They are invaluable not only for statistics, industry personnel, and the like, but also for polemical essays on the state of the cinema and the industry (particularly in the early volumes). They provide a valuable snapshot of the industry in a given year.

Senjika eiga shiryō: Eiga nenkan Shōwa 18, 19, 20-nen, edited by Tokyo Kokuritsu Kindai Bijutsukan Firumu Sentā
Tokyo: Nihon Tosho Sentā, 2006.
東京国立近代美術館フィルムセンター監修『戦時下映画資料　映画年鑑昭和18・19・20年』日本図書センター, 2006.

A reprint of the original manuscripts (some still in handwritten form) for three wartime film yearbooks that were never published.

The Rest

Eiga bideo iyābukku = Film & video yearbook
Tokyo: Kinema Junpōsha, 1990-1999.
『映画ビデオイヤーブック＝Film & video yearbook』キネマ旬報社, 1990-1999.

Kinema Junpōsha's yearbook for the 1990s (see the more detailed annotation below, p. 93) that concentrates on introducing the films of each year.

Eiga iyābukku, edited by Etō Tsutomu
Tokyo: Shakai Shisōsha, 1991-.
江藤努編『映画イヤーブック』社会思想社, 1991-.

Another short-lived yearbook centered on introducing individual films, published between 1991 and 1998. It can contain more critical reviews than similar yearbooks as well as lists of V-cinema.

Eiga jōei katsudō nenkan: Chiiki ni okeru eiga jōei jōkyō chōsa
Tokyo: Kokusai Bunka Kōryū Suishin Kyōkai (Ace Japan), 2004-.
『映画上映活動年鑑　地域における映画上映状況調査』国際文化交流推進協会(エース・ジャパン), 2004-.

This irregularly published yearbook is a gold mine of data on the exhibition system in Japan. It is one of a number of important publications by the Japan Community Cinema Center, whose membership includes all the festivals and mini-theaters in Japan that are devoted to film culture outside of the major distribution networks. Contents change from issue to issue, but include remarkably detailed analysis of the exhibition situation from prefecture to prefecture.

Eigakan, edited by Toeda Hirokazu
Tokyo: Yumani Shobō, 2006.
十重田裕一編集『映画館』ゆまに書房, 2006.

Primarily a fine reprint from the Korekushon modan toshi bunka series of the 800-page *1929-1930 Motion Picture Year Book* (*Nihon eiga jigyō sōran*), from Ichikawa Sai's Kokusai Eiga Tsūshinsha, this is an invaluable resource for studying pre-1930 exhibition and distribution. This mostly supersedes the previous issues in 1925, 1926, and 1928, as much of its data covers previous years. It is also included in Makino Mamoru and Iwamoto Kenji's *Eiga nenkan—Showa-hen I* (see above); however, this Yumani version contains invaluable supplements in the back, starting with an appendix with an array of supplemental charts and figures reprinted from other sources. In addition to this, there is an excellent *kaisetsu,* bibliography, and a wonderful 1895-1945 timeline that indexes journal articles on exhibition practices.

Japanese Film
Tokyo: UniJapan Film, 1958-.

This long-running English-language yearbook has been printed every year in March by UniJapan, the non-profit organization that is charged with promoting Japanese movies abroad. It is thus largely a promotional catalog, one that for many years tended to feature the works more of major studios than independents, but it has become more expansive in recent years and also includes industry statistics and contact addresses for the major players.

Nihon eiga, edited by Satō Tadao and Yamane Sadao
Tokyo: Haga Shoten, 1976-1985.
佐藤忠男、山根貞男編集『日本映画』芳賀書店, 1976-1985.

This short-lived yearbook may have a lot of pictures, but it also has good critical essays that provide an image of Japanese film culture in those years. Published between 1976 and 1985.

PR eiga nenkan
Tokyo: Nihon Shōken Tōshi Kyōkai, 1959-1967.
『PR映画年鑑』日本証券投資協会, 1959-1967.

This is a yearbook devoted exclusively to the PR (public relations) film, which prospered in the booming 1950s. Typical to the form, the *PR eiga nenkan* provides lists of producers and halls (including their rates). However, the main attraction is the list of films that includes producers, running times, dates of completion, synopses, and other data. The 1960 issue folds the content of 1959 into its pages, and purports to list pre-1959 films. The *nenkan* is useful for seeing the scope of PR film production just as it is serving as a petri dish for independent documentary film talent. The filmographies are surely not complete, and the criteria for inclusion goes unstated.

Encyclopedias and Dictionaries

Film encyclopedias and dictionaries are fundamental to the discipline, attempting to offer standard definitions of terms and frameworks for thinking about basic concepts. Unfortunately, such encyclopedias have been rare in Japan—again a mark of the poor state of film studies—appearing at a rate of about one a decade. The result is a lack of vigorous discussion about fundamental terms and concepts, even though some texts, such as Bijutsu Shuppansha's two film encyclopedias, can be quite polemical. For the foreign scholar, these works can offer, beyond basic definitions and information, a picture of how the discipline is being shaped in Japan.

The Best of the Best

Sekai eiga daijiten, edited by Iwamoto Kenji and Takamura Kuratarō
Tokyo: Nihon Tosho Sentā, 2008.
岩本憲児、高村倉太郎監修『世界映画大事典』日本図書センター, 2008.

Ten years in the making, this is the most extensive encyclopedia of film published in Japanese to date. It covers the entirety of world cinema, so entries on Japan are in the minority. However, it's a very thick book with 4,000 entries written by the major figures in film studies in Japan. The editors made superior decisions in defining their entries. Aside from the old standards like genres, studios and famous directors, there are Japan-related entries on criticism and theory, institutions like the *benshi*, film movements, critical debates, government policy, censorship, film festivals, and much more. The coverage of the rest of Asia, South America and Africa is a helpful corrective to the inexcusably Eurocentric English-language film encyclopedias. An accompanying volume contains a multi-lingual chart of film terminology, timelines, and helpful indexes.

The Best

The Anime Encyclopedia: A Guide to Japanese Animation Since 1917, by Jonathan Clements and Helen McCarthy
Berkeley, Calif.: Stone Bridge Press, revised and expanded version, 2006.

At over 3,000 indexed and cross-referenced entries, this is a rather monumental effort to list all the major animated films from the Taishō era to the present. Entries include production data, dates, some credits, and synopses; the latter are basically witty reviews and have disenchanted anime fans whose favorite films get panned. The book itself is compiled and written by fans, so their standards of quality are fittingly loose. Regrettably, this also means that dates, episode counts, transliterations, plot descriptions, names—what else is there?—are not to be trusted. It is also inevitably weighted towards recent works. That said, it is an essential reference guide for the world of Japanese animation.

The Encyclopedia of Pop Culture, by Mark Schilling
New York: Weatherhill, 1997.

An excellent resource on popular culture, weighted heavily on the 1960s and beyond. It's barely thick enough to constitute an "encyclopedia" and the style may be chatty, but this is a serious work of scholarship on the most prominent genres, stars, and phenomena in Japanese pop culture.

The Midnight Eye Guide to New Japanese Film, by Tom Mes and Jasper Sharp
Berkeley: Stone Bridge Press, 2005.

A paper complement to the *Midnight Eye* website (160), this guide to contemporary Japanese film includes excellent profiles of 20 directors and lively analyses of nearly 100 films. While selective in coverage, the decisions on what to cover and what to leave out where smartly made.

The Rest

Eiga hyakka jiten = Encyclopedia of cinema, edited by Iwasaki Akira, et al.
Tokyo: Hakuyōsha, 1954.
岩崎昶他編纂『映画百科辞典 = Encyclopedia of cinema』白揚社, 1954.

This encyclopedia was edited by a number of luminaries in the postwar film world, including Iwasaki Akira, Tanikawa Yoshio, Miyajima Yoshio, and Imai Tadashi. While the majority of its entries are now superfluous—especially with the publication of *Sekai eiga daijiten* (88)—this remains a good resource for definitions of technical terms circa the 1950s. At the very least, it is an interesting specimen of how cinema was conceptualized at the time.

Eiga no jiten
Tokyo: Gōdō Shuppan, 1978.
山田和夫監修、映画の事典編集委員会編『映画の事典』合同出版, 1978.

Marxist critic and historian Yamada Kazuo managed this impressive project. It features the usual brief bios (which include staff members), conversion charts, and technical term definitions of the typical dictionary. However, the main value of this book is its collection of historical documents. Always interested in the relationship of the film industry and state power, Yamada anthologizes a wealth of government documents. They include various government regulations, landmark censorship cases, and a particularly nice selection of directives from the American Occupation.

Eiga shōjiten, edited by Hasumi Shigehiko, et al.
Tokyo: Esso Sekiyu Kōhōbu, 1985.
蓮実重彦他編著『映画小事典』エッソ石油広報部, 1985.

A really tiny book: 15 cm tall, only 144 pages—on really thin pages. And also published by an oil company. But it contains entries written by some of the top film critics in the 1980s and represents a creative tweaking of the concept of "dictionary." Rather than attempting a measured description of important terminology or figures, you might call this an inventory of cinematic tropes: asphalt, steps, kiss, entryway, rain, hand—all traced through different cinematic cultures and periods. Quite a few entries are also specific to Japanese film, such as tatami, *ninja*, or ricksha. In any case, we include this slight volume among the bricks for the access it provides to an influential group of critics' approach to cinema, as well as the further evidence of the creativity of Japanese film's rich print culture.

Engeki eiga terebi buyō opera hyakka = Pocket book of theatrical arts, edited by Kurahashi Takeshi and Takeuchi Toshiharu
Tokyo: Heibonsha, 1983.
倉橋健, 竹内敏晴監修『演劇映画テレビ舞踊オペラ百科 = Pocket book of theatrical arts』平凡社, 1983.

Not the best of dictionaries—many of the entries are too short—but sufficient for a quick search.

Gendai eiga jiten, edited by Okada Susumu, et al.
Tokyo: Bijutsu Shuppansha, 1973.
岡田晋他編集執筆『現代映画事典』美術出版社, 1973.

The first attempt at a real film studies dictionary, it is now somewhat outdated. But since there are a small number of entries, each one is broader and longer and written by major figures like Satō Tadao, Matsumoto Toshio, Sasaki Kiichi, Hani Susumu, and Iwasaki Akira.

Katsudō shashin hyakka hōten, by Umeya Shōkichi
Tokyo: Umemiya Shōkichi, 1911.
梅屋庄吉著『活動寫眞百科寶典』梅屋庄吉, 1911.

While essentially a catalog of films available at M. Pathé, the film company headed by the adventuresome Umeya Shōkichi, it is presented as an encyclopedia of human knowledge, with films categorized according to the various fields of science and research. It is as if cinema—and Umemiya—are being presented here as the treasure trove of modern knowledge. Reprinted in volume 23 of the *Nihon eigaron gensetsu taikei* (78).

Kinema handobukku: Eiga jiten, edited by Kawazoe Toshimoto
Tokyo: Shūhōkaku, 1925.
川添利基編『キネマハンドブック　映畫辭典』聚芳閣, 1925.

While there are other dictionaries from the prewar period, this one was published at a particularly interesting moment in Japanese film history, when the meanings of many terms were being debated and codified.

Nihon no anime zenshi: Sekai o seishita Nihon anime no kiseki, by Yamaguchi Yasuo
Tokyo: Ten Bukkusu, 2004.
山口康男著『日本のアニメ全史 世界を制した日本アニメの奇跡』テン・ブックス, 2004.

Yamaguchi's appendixes include a glossary of technical terms for animation. Many of the entries are *katakana* loan words from English, but the meanings are specific to this production culture. Anyone doing serious work on anime, especially translators, would find this glossary extremely helpful. (For the full entry on Yamaguchi's book see p. 139.)

Shin eiga jiten, edited by Asanuma Keiji, et al.
Tokyo: Bijutsu Shuppansha, 1980.
浅沼圭司他編集『新映画事典』美術出版社, 1980.

A revised version of the 1973 *Gendai eiga jiten* with new or re-written entries and additional writers like Hasumi Shigehiko, Asanuma Keiji, and Hatano Tetsurō.

Taishū bunka jiten = Encyclopedia of popular culture, edited by Ishikawa Hiroyoshi, et al.
Tokyo: Kōbundō, 1991.
石川弘義他編集委員『大衆文化事典 = Encyclopedia of popular culture』弘文堂, 1991.

An excellent encyclopedia of various forms of Japanese popular culture, including the cinema. Each entry includes a bibliography, so one can sometimes start research with this text. There are still not enough film entries, however.

Translation of Film, Video Terms into Japanese, by Verne Carlson
Burbank, Calif.: Double C Publication, 1984.

This Japanese-(American) English dictionary covers nearly any technical term one might come across for any stage of film production, from preproduction to post. It's designed for clueless Hollywood producers traveling to Japan to work, so it uses a peculiar style of transliteration in the hope that anyone could come up with a beautiful Japanese pronunciation. The back of the book also lists a few commonly used phrases in filmmaking, our favorites being "Are there *experienced* personnel?" and "This will not do."

Filmographies

General filmographies are reference books that specialize in providing filmographic information for a broad range of individual cinematic works: cast and staff credits, release dates, length, and in some cases, plot summaries, technical data, name of opening theater, and even commentary. Given the sheer volume of films made in Japan, however, few of these general filmographies offer extensive cast and staff information (including character names). For that you have to search out the Kinema junpō *introductions (*shōkai*) or more specialized filmographies (by director, actor, and the like). You can consult postwar* Kinema junpō shōkai *and the Japanese Movie Database on the internet, but since they can contain errors, filmographic information should always be checked against other published sources or the film itself.*

The Best

The Asian Film Library Reference to Japanese Film, edited by Stephen Cremin
London: The Asian Film Library, 1998.

Although it looks rather suspicious, bound as it is in a ringed binder, this is rightly a core reference book for Japanese film. It is divided into two volumes: "Films" and "Names." The 2,259 film entries render titles in *kanji,* roman letters, and English translation (although there are no alternative release titles). This is followed by basic credits and a minimal amount of data. Names with entries in the second volume are in bold, and turning to those entries one finds filmographies for well over 3,000 people. Cremin has impressively included hundreds of staff entries above and beyond all the directors and actors. Transliterations for the names appear reasonably reliable, although they use no macrons. It's impressive and useful, but ultimately a slim selection considering the scale of Japanese film production. The silent era gets particularly short shrift here. Nevertheless, as one of the few transliterized name and title indexes, this reference is a must-have resource for those without Japanese reading skills.

A Critical Handbook of Japanese Film Directors: From the Silent Era to the Present Day, by Alexander Jacoby
Berkeley, Calif.: Stone Bridge Press, 2008.

Alexander Jacoby's handbook provides biographical sketches and filmographies for about 150 directors. Most are feature filmmakers, although the most prominent documentary directors are also included. The filmographies are painstakingly researched and checked for accuracy. While the selection is minimal compared to the other books in this category, the book stands apart for the biographies. They are lengthy and critical, based as they are on extensive viewing.

Eiga bideo iyābukku = Film & video yearbook
Tokyo: Kinema Junpōsha, 1990-1999.
『映画ビデオイヤーブック=Film & video yearbook』キネマ旬報社, 1990-1999.

A continuation of the Kinema Junpōsha project of recording all the films made or released in Japan (see below). By this time, the publication had turned into an annual yearbook, an essential tool for grasping the cinema of the 1990s. The project was sadly discontinued after the 1999 volume.

FC: Firumu Sentā
Tokyo: Tōkyō Kokuritsu Kindai Bijitsukan Firumu Sentā, 1971-1993.
『FC: フィルムセンター』東京国立近代美術館フィルムセンター, 1971-1993.

FC was the series of catalogs that the National Film Center published for each of its special programs between 1971 and 1993. While these could contain essays, the core of each catalog was a detailed filmography, usually one page long, for each film shown, including credits, a plot summary, and historical commentary. Since the NFC staff generally wrote these, the filmographies here are some of the most thorough and accurate ones published in Japanese.

The Japanese Filmography: A Complete Reference to 209 Filmmakers and the Over 1250 Films Released in the United States, 1900 Through 1994, by Stuart Galbraith IV
Jefferson, N.C.: McFarland, 1996.

This is a significant work for those who cannot read Japanese. For those who can use the reference books from Japan, it's still essential for the complete data on U.S. release titles and dates. Galbraith also lists video releases, although this part becomes less useful with each passing year and with technological innovation (Galbraith's book was published on the cusp of the DVD revolution, and ours on the switch to HD).

Kurashikku eiga nyūsu
Tokyo: Musei Eiga Kanshōkai.
『クラシック映画ニュース』無声映画鑑賞会.

The Musei Eiga Kanshōkai (Friends of Silent Film Association) has been showing silent films in Tokyo with *benshi* accompaniment at least once a month for about 50 years. *Kurashikku eiga nyūsu (Classic Cinema News)* is basically the program handed out at each screening as well as mailed to Association members. It may be tiny, but it contains detailed cast/credit information and plot synopses of each of the works shown that month, in addition to star bios, short reminisces by members, and Association news. Although many films get repeated in the 600-plus issues they have printed so far, it is still a valuable resource of information on silent and prewar cinema.

Nihon eiga sakuhin jiten/Complete Dictionary of Japanese Movies from 1896 to 1945 August, edited by Nihon Eigashi Kenkyūkai.
Tokyo: Kagaku Shoin, 1996.
日本映画史研究会編『日本映画作品辞典　戦前篇 = Complete dictionary of Japanese movies from 1896 to 1945 August』科学書院: 発売元 霞ケ関出版株式会社, 1996.
Nihon eiga sakuhin jiten/Complete Dictionary of Japanese Movies from 1945 August to 1988 December, edited by Nihon Eigashi Kenkyūkai.
Tokyo: Kagaku Shoin, 1998.
日本映画史研究会編『日本映画作品辞典　戦後篇 = Complete dictionary of Japanese movies from 1945 August to 1988 December』科学書院: 発売元 霞ケ関出版株式会社, 1998.

This massive dictionary of films and filmmakers takes up an entire bookshelf and is an indispensable tool for Japanese cinema studies. A project run by the Nihon Eigashi Kenkyūkai, it is an attempt to list every film and filmmaker in Japan (other related Kagaku Shoin projects cover staff and actors as well foreign films shown in Japan [see pp. 99-100 and 104-105]). Much of the information is culled from only three sources—*Kinema junpō*, *Kura-*

shikku eiga nyūsu, and government censorship records—but this is by far the most reliable resource for identifying release dates and filmographies on this scale. It is composed of two six-volume sections on prewar and postwar Japanese films (the other publications on prewar and postwar foreign films, Japanese actors and staff, and foreign actors are cross-referenced when possible). For some sense of the coverage, the Japanese section on staff members lists 16,441 people, eight times that of the *Kinema junpō* reference dictionary. (For our entry on the biographical dictionary volumes, see pp. 104-105.) This series also represents an important first step for entering the archive. Because Japanese film periodicals are so poorly indexed, one must often browse through volumes page-by-page. Entries here give exact release dates, which makes trolling for articles much more expeditious, as you can begin by pulling journals around that date. Prewar listings also indicate first-run theaters, which allows one to navigate collections of theater programs. Finally, all titles and personal names are thankfully rendered in *hiragana,* although one should always cross-check readings when possible. Do note, however, that given the size of the project, each filmographic entry is rather short, only listing some personnel and a limited number of cast members without character names. Given the selectiveness of the filmography, one cannot assume that the filmographies given for actors and other individuals are complete. These works are thus most helpful for core information, not for full filmographies.

Nihon eiga sakuhin taikan: Eiga bunkenshi hajimete no sakuhin zenshū
Tokyo: Kinema Junpōsha, 1960-1961.
『日本映画作品大鑑　映画文献史初めての作品全集』キネマ旬報社，1960-1961.

This is the first comprehensive listing of the 33,500 or so films released in Japan, both foreign and Japanese, both feature and some shorts, up until 1945. It was compiled by Kinema Junpōsha, the publisher of the trade journal that has long made an effort to record every film produced and/or released in Japan. Kinema Junpōsha books tend to set the standard for filmographies and biographic dictionaries, but this relatively early project does contain many errors. The filmography also lists films in order of release without an index, and so it is difficult to use. The National Film Center used to have a catalog in which each entry was basically cut and pasted onto an index card and then filed in *gojūonjun* order. Given that the cast and credit information is as limited as the Kagaku Shoin books, its usefulness has been superseded by that work except for the fact it does note which issues of *Kinema junpō* contain an introduction (*shōkai*) to each film. This and the subsequent works constitute Kinema Junpōsha's effort to catalog in book form all the films made in Japan.

Nihon eiga sakuhin zenshū
Tokyo: Kinema Junpōsha, 1973.
『日本映画作品全集』キネマ旬報社, 1973.

In some ways a continuation of the *Taikan's* project, this work attempts to cover the 9,932 Japanese films released from the end of the war to the end of 1972. All the films are listed in *gojūonjun* order in a 128-page section with very limited filmographic information and the *KineJun* number where the *shōkai* was printed. In another section, 1,893 of those films (plus 454 prewar works) deemed of artistic merit are introduced in *gojūonjun* order through short commentaries written by major critics. A very handy tool if you are working with postwar film or searching through *Kinema junpō* for reviews and articles (which tend to be printed in or near the *shōkai* issue).

Pia cinema club, Nihon eiga hen
Tokyo: Pia.
『ぴあシネマクラブ日本映画編』ぴあ

Basically a film viewer's guide published yearly with short introductions to many films—kind of like Leonard Maltin's *Movie Guide*, only physically bigger and without the evaluative reviews (early versions did have critical reviews). A helpful book for confirming the readings of titles (not always accurate, but a good start) and VHS/DVD availability. Also contains indexes by actor and staff member. Since it is cheaper than many of the other reference books, anyone serious about Japanese film study should personally own a copy.

Pia cinema club, gaikoku eiga hen
Tokyo: Pia.
『ぴあシネマクラブ外国映画編』ぴあ

The volume for foreign films. It can also provide a quick reference for confirming Japanese titles of foreign films or the original title of a foreign film for which you only know the Japanese title.

Sekai eiga sakuhin kiroku zenshū
Tokyo: Kinema Junpōsha, 1975-.
『世界映画作品・記録全集』キネマ旬報社, 1975-.

The continuation of *Nihon eiga sakuhin zenshū* and its foreign film sibling, now taking on the form of a film biennial that includes both cinemas. These volumes, which continue until 1989, thus serve both as filmographies and as yearbooks on the state of the industry. They also provide the *KineJun* issue number for the *shōkai* of each film.

The Rest

A Critical History and Filmography of Toho's Godzilla Series, by David Kalat
Jefferson, N.C.: McFarland & Co., 1997.

A filmography with lengthy historical analyses of every Godzilla film up to the 1995 *Godzilla vs Destroyer* (*Gojira vs. Desutoroia*). An abundance of esoterica makes this a very fun reference book.

Eiga hyakunen: Eiga wa kō shite hajimatta, edited by Yomiuri Shinbun Bunkabu
Tokyo: Kinema Junpōsha, 1997.
読売新聞文化部編『映画百年　映画はこうして始まった』キネマ旬報社, 1997.

See annotation on pp. 109-110.

Eiga eizō gyōkai shūshoku gaido
Tokyo: Kinema Junpōsha, 2008-.
『映画映像業界就職ガイド』キネマ旬報社, 2008-.

This may be a primer for getting an industry job, but the guidebook and directory on Japanese film and television companies is very useful in that it gives more information than the Green Book (103). It's updated every year.

Eiga, terebi dorama, gensaku bungei dēta bukku, by Etō Shigehiro
Tokyo: Bensei Shuppan, 2005.
江藤茂博著『映画、テレビドラマ、原作文芸データブック』ベンセイ出版, 2005.

This is a fascinating collection of filmographies for authors, listing all the adaptations of their work into both film and television. We intended to provide the number of adaptations Etō lists for Kurama Tengu, but kept losing count there were so many. One-hundred and twenty authors are represented, but their selection seems almost arbitrary. Etō's criterion seems to be the popularity of the adaptations as opposed to the reputation of the original works. This helps explain exclusions like Nagai Kafū, Abe Kōbō, Murakamis Ryū and Haruki—the list goes on and on. That said, nearly every filmography includes works (especially television programs) that one might not discover otherwise. The Nichigai Associates *gensaku* dictionary tends to be more thorough for films (100).

Japan in Film: A Comprehensive Annotated Catalogue of Documentary and Theatrical Films on Japan Available in the United States, edited by Peter Grilli
New York: Japan Society, 1984.

The book's subtitle pretty much says it all: this is "A Comprehensive Annotated Catalogue of Documentary and Theatrical Films on Japan Available in the United States." Grilli's book lists well over 600 films, 130 of which are feature films. Each entry has data, credits, synopsis, a rating, and distribution information. Granted, many of the distributors are either defunct or have let their contracts expire. However, plenty are still in business, and most of the documentaries are held by the 49 university collections Grilli trolled for titles. We have found WorldCat extremely unreliable for 16mm film, so *Japan in Film* provides the best sense for what English-subtitled prints are available (at least as of 1984).

Japanese Cinema: The Essential Handbook, by Thomas Weisser and Yuko Mihara Weisser
Miami, FL: Vital Books, 5th ed., 2003.

There's something more palatable about the Weissers' work when delimited by low genre categories, as in the two encyclopedias below. Here the knee-jerk anti-intellectualism is more jarring, the mistakes and elisions more unforgivable. And if you actually buy these books, the redundancies across the volumes become grating. It's got good pictures.

Japanese Cinema Encyclopedia: The Horror, Fantasy, SciFi Films, by Thomas Weisser and Yuko Mihara Weisser
Miami, FL: Vital Books, 1997.

This companion to the Weissers' filmography of sex films covers 1955-1997, everything from *Godzilla* to *Roaming Tortured Brain*. As with *The Sex Films*, the English language titles and dates are unreliable, and the film data minimal and researchers would do well to skip straight to the Galbraith (see below). However, the Weissers' taste is more . . . catholic; Galbraith tends to ignore exploitation films and includes none of this book's crazily charming photographs.

Japanese Cinema Encyclopedia: The Sex Films, by Thomas Weisser and Yuko Mihara Weisser
Miami, FL: Vital Books, 1998.

Two inches of pink film synopses—someone had to do it. The book covers

1963-1998; but is limited by the slimness of the information, as only title, date, studio and minimal credit information is listed. The main attraction is undoubtedly the inclusion of short plot synopses with reference to historical context (not to mention the conventional star rating system!). Use with caution, as the dating, titling, and English translations of pink films are notoriously unreliable.

Japanese Films: A Filmography and Commentary, 1921-1989, by Beverly Buehrer
Jefferson, N.C.: McFarland & Co., 1990.

This book includes lengthy plot synopses, some commentary, and basic credit information for 86 mainstream films. The selection feels strangely canonical and arbitrary at the same time, probably because it is such a small number of films. There is a good bibliography of English books in back, important for its inclusion of periodical articles.

Japanese Science Fiction, Fantasy and Horror Films: A Critical Analysis of 103 Features Released in the United States, 1950-1992, by Stuart Galbraith IV
Jefferson, N.C.: McFarland & Co., 2007.

Stuart Galbraith IV provides a model filmography with this book, although it lacks the bibliographic information of the Mizoguchi book listed above. The bulk of the Galbraith's project consists of 103 synopses that provide historical context and critical reception for his canon of fantastic films (1950-1992). The back of the book contains a proper filmography, structured by studio and including release titles, domestic and foreign release dates, ratings, running times, and full credits. Unfortunately, the only difference between the original 1994 version and this edition is the price.

Hakurai kinema sakuhin jiten: Nihon de senzen ni jōei sareta gaikoku eiga ichiran = Complete dictionary of imported movies up to 1945 August, edited by Sekai Eigashi Kenkyūkai
Tokyo: Kagaku Shoin, 1997.
世界映画史研究会編『舶来キネマ作品辞典　日本で戦前に上映された外国映画一覧 = Complete dictionary of imported movies upto 1945 August』科学書院: 発売元 霞ヶ関出版, 1997.
Hakurai kinema sakuhin jiten. Sengo hen. 1: Nihon de sengo (1945-1988) ni jōei sareta gaikoku eiga ichiran (1)
Tokyo: Kagaku Shoin, 2004.

世界映画史研究会編者『舶来キネマ作品辞典. 戦後篇. 1: 日本で戦後(1945-1988)に上映された外国映画一覧(1)』科学書院: 発売元霞ヶ関出版, 2004.

These two multi-volume works itemizing foreign film exhibition share the plusses and limitations of the other Kagaku Shoin dictionaries (see pp. 94-95 and 104-105), but can be especially helpful with both release dates and Japanese titles and original titles of foreign films, especially for works not covered by *Pia*. This is cross-referenced with a large dictionary of foreign actors we do not include in this bibliography.

Nihon eiga gensaku jiten = Original works of Japanese films
Tokyo: Nichigai Asoshiētsu: Hatsubaimoto Kinokuniya Shoten, 2007.
スティングレイ・日外アソシエーツ共編『日本映画原作事典 = Original works of Japanese films』日外アソシエーツ：発売元紀伊國屋書店, 2007.

Generally more thorough than Etō's work (p. 97), this is ordered by film title with an index by title of the original work. A plus is that it includes publication information for the original and sometimes plot summaries that are not found in Etō. It does not, however, include an author index.

Nihon kyōiku eiga sōmokuroku, edited by Zen Nihon Eiga Kyōiku Kenkyūkai
Osaka: Osaka Mainichi Shinbunsha, 1937.
全日本映画教育研究会編『日本教育映画総目録』大阪毎日新聞社, 1937.

This relatively short list came with the January 1937 issue of *Eiga kyōiku*. It does, however, give a sense for the wide variety of educational documentaries of the era.

Nihon tanpen eizō shūsaku mokuroku: Eizō sakuhin de miru Nihon no 100-nen
Tokyo: Eizō Bunka Seisakusha Renmei, 1999.
『日本短編映像秀作目録　映像作品で見る日本の100年』映像文化製作者連盟: 発売 紀伊國屋書店, 1999.

This book lists 5,000 non-theatrical films, mostly from the postwar era. It begins with a list of 100 deemed the most important in the century of cinema before the book was published. This is a contentious list to be sure. The book was put out by the Eizō Bunka Seisakusha Renmei, which was founded in 1953 and endured some controversies in the subsequent decades. Put it this way: you won't find any of the famous political documentaries of the New Left here. The remaining sections do, however, list award-winning films for a given year, and the 171 members of the Renmei (with their contact information and the five films each is most proud of).

Nihon nyūsu eigashi: Kaisen zen'ya kara shūsen chokugo made
Tokyo: Mainichi Shinbunsha, 1980.
『日本ニュース映画史　開戦前夜から終戦直後まで』毎日新聞社, 1980.

During WWII, all newsreels were consolidated into a single series called *Nihon nyūsu*. Although the films and rights fell to NHK after the war, Mainichi produced a wonderful visual index of the run (1940-1945) as part of their Ichiokunin no Shōwa shi series. In addition to curt descriptions of the content, there is a page or more of frame blow-ups from each of the 264 issues. These can be particularly useful when trying to look at the films at institutions like the Kawasaki City Museum (14-15) and the Shōwa-kan (47-48).

Nihon tokusatsu, gensō eiga zenshū
Tokyo: Asahi Sonorama, 2005.
『日本特撮、幻想映画全集』朝日ソノラマ, 2005.

A revised and expanded version of the 1997 book published by Keibunsha, this data-heavy tome lists 857 special effects films from the period 1948 to 2004, all organized by decade. Its devotion to data would make any SF *otaku* proud. Notes video releases.

Senzen Nihon eiga sōmokuroku
Osaka: Nihon Eiga Kenkyūkai, 1994.
『戦前日本映画総目録』日本映画研究会, 1994.

This is a self-published list of feature films produced from 1931-1945. It is incomplete and thus no substitute for *The Complete Dictionary of Japanese Movies* (94-95). However, films are listed by year and grouped by studio, making it useful for seeing the major films of a given studio or production company in a given year. A curious chart in the back separates out and quantifies the 5,544 films by *gendaigeki* vs. *jidaigeki* and 16 genres.

Tōhō SF tokusatsu eiga shirīzu
Tokyo: Tōhō, 1985-.
『東宝SF特撮映画シリーズ』東宝, 1985-.

A series of over a dozen A4-sized glossy paperback books covering many of the major Tōhō scifi or *kaijū* movies not just with pictures, but with pretty thorough documentation, including the scripts, pressbooks, storyboards, and ad material.

USIS eiga mokuroku
Tokyo: Tokyo Beikoku Taishikan Eigabu Haikyūka, 1953-1966.
『USIS映画目録1955』東京米国大使館映画部配給課, 1953-1966.

During the postwar Occupation, the American government used short films to inculcate Japanese into the ways of democracy—at least as they saw it. These films were widely seen, as Markus explains in *Forest of Pressure* (138). They are also sprinkled across Japan in prefectural libraries and the most unlikely places. He once stumbled upon a cache of the films, complete with bilingual screening guides produced by the Americans, in what amounted to a broom closet at Tokushima Prefectural Archives. We have also seen collections in other city and prefectural libraries. Published after the Occupation of the mainland, this series of indexes published irregularly between 1953 and 1966 gives a sense for the titles the Americans distributed across the country. There are not too many copies of this index around, but we suspect the actual films are easier to find than one would think. Presumably, NARA (19-21) also holds copies of everything.

Yoshizawa Shōten catalogs
吉澤商店定價表

Yoshizawa and Co. was the most prominent of the four major film importers and producers in the early cinema era and one sign of that was their publishing activities, which included the magazines *Katsudō shashinkai* and a series of catalogs displaying their wares, which included not only films, but lantern slides and machines. The catalogs appeared under various names, but years 1905-1910 (Meiji 38-43) are collected in the second volume of Makino Mamoru's *Meiji eizō bunken shiryō shūsei* (Tokyo: Yumani Shobō, 2006), which itself is part of the *Nihon eigaron gensetsu taikei* (78). That volume also includes a 1912 catalog from the Tsūzoku Kyōiku Chōsa Iinkai. Aside from the list of films, the catalogs provide film lengths and include descriptions both long and short.

Biographical Dictionaries

These dictionaries are useful for obtaining name readings, personal data, filmographies, and sometimes critical commentary. Kinema Junpōsha again sets the standard for reference materials on individuals involved in film production, but Nichigai Asoshiētsu has helped fill in some of the gaps Kinema Junpōsha left. The first bio-

graphical dictionaries unfortunately only focused on directors and actors, making it difficult to look up other people involved in film production. Nichigai has recently produced dictionaries that include other (but not all) members of the film crew. Users should be aware that even the better biographical dictionaries are not always accurate, especially given how marginal film culture has been in Japan. For name readings and other data, it is best to always check two or three different sources.

The Best

Eiga haiyū jiten: Senzen Nihon-hen, by Moriuchi Masashi
Tokyo: Miraisha, 1994.
森内政志著『映画俳優事典　戦前日本編』未来社, 1994.

This is one of the better biographical dictionaries. Moriuchi based this book on a series of nearly 500 biographies he wrote for *Kurashikku eiga nyūsu* (94). As original, signed pieces of writing—as opposed to typically anonymous and dull entries—they are a bit longer than the usual dictionary and are far more interesting to read. Unfortunately for us, he never got to his postwar edition.

Eizō media sakka jinmei jiten
Tokyo: Nichigai Asoshiētsu, 1991.
日外アソシエーツ編集『映像メディア作家人名事典』日外アソシエーツ: 発売元 紀伊國屋書店, 1991.

Now largely superseded by *Nihon no eigajin* (106), this is still quite valuable because it includes not only directors and actors, but also many other personnel that are ignored by the major dictionaries. It is thus good for looking up producers, screenwriters, cinematographers, and the like. Like many of the Nichigai dictionaries, the writing is cold and dictionary-like, unlike the *KineJun* works; however, each entry provides name readings, a basic biography and filmography.

Geinōkai shinshiroku: Geinō techō
Tokyo: Rengō Tsūshinsha, 1973-.
『芸能界紳士録　芸能手帳』連合通信社, 1973-.

Known in the film, television and record industries as the "Green Book" (guess why), this is the main address book for production companies, studios, talent agencies and the like. It's updated yearly, and is extremely expensive. This also means you can often pick up old copies at the used book stores for a steep discount. Along with their "Red Book" (*Tarento meiboroku*, 107), this is the best way to find contact information for artists.

Meiji-Shōwa shoki haiyū meikan shūsei
Tokyo: Yumani Shobō, 2005.
『明治・昭和初期俳優名鑑集成』ゆまに書房, 2005.

A 14-volume reprint of prewar actor directories—covering performers on screen and on stage—including such series as *Nihon eiga haiyū meikan.* A treasure-trove of images (since these were mainly sold to fans), but also a valuable testimony to fan culture of the era.

Nihon eigajin kaimei besshō jiten, edited by Nagata Tetsurō
Tokyo: Kokusho Kankōkai, 2004.
永田哲朗編『日本映画人改名・別称事典』国書刊行会, 2004.

Film people change their names for all sorts of reasons. Their birth name lacks pizzazz. They come from the theater and took their teacher's name. They use stage names as pseudonyms to hide work in television or original video productions. They signify the end of a career slump with a new name. They get bored. A fortuneteller tells them to. Whatever the reason, it is not unusual to see two or three name changes over the course of a career. *Nihon eigajin kaimei besshō jiten* is a name dictionary just for those who have worked under more than one moniker. It started out as a column in *Ōsaka eiga kyōiku,* a fan newspaper from Kansai. Then Nagata expanded it to book form, covering over 3,600 names (for far less individuals, naturally). A complete index in the back makes for easy navigation through the bewildering proliferation of name changes.

Nihon eiga haiyū zenshi, by Inomata Katsuhito and Tayama Rikiya
Tokyo: Shakai Shisōsha, 1977-1986.
猪俣勝人、田山力也著『日本映画俳優全史』社会思想社, 1977-1986.

As a *bunko-ban,* this is a biographical dictionary you could easily acquire for your own shelf. There are three volumes, one for men, another for women, and a third added in 1986 (edited only by Tayama) for young actors in their teens and twenties. Each volume is divided into two parts, representing the authors' A- and B-lists. Entries are short glosses, although they do give a sense for the qualities audiences valued in these stars. The authors also list key works for their A-list actors. Most of the filmographies were not updated after the first edition.

Nihon eiga jinmei jiten: Haiyū hen / Complete Dictionary of Actors and Actresses in Japan
Tokyo: Kagaku Shoin, 2005.

日本映画史研究会編『日本映画人名辞典　俳優篇 = Complete dictionary of actors and actresses in Japan』科学書院: 発売元霞ケ関出版, 2005.
Nihon eiga jinmei jiten: Sutaffu-hen / Complete Dictionary of Movie Staffs in Japan, edited by Nihon Eigashi Kenkyūkai
Tokyo: Kagaku Shoin, 2005.
日本映画史研究会編『日本映画人名辞典・スタッフ編 = Complete dictionary of movie staffs in Japan』科学書院:発売元霞ヶ関出版, 2005.

These massive dictionaries of actors and filmmakers boasts a listing of over 11,000 actors, far more than the 4,500 featured in the most recent *KineJun* actor dictionaries, and over 16,000 staff members. However, the Kagaku Shoin dictionaries only list the films for each performer; the only personal information is dates of birth and death. It does, however, attempt name and film title readings, and database numbering refers you to the entries in the Kagaku Shoin filmographies. The film listings for each individual thus depend on what cast/credit information was inputted in the Japanese filmographies; since those were sometimes limited, the lists for individuals can thus be incomplete for many personnel. Still, a quite useful work for getting a start at name readings for less famous individuals not found in other dictionaries (though it is not certain where these readings were confirmed).

Nihon eiga jinmei jiten (*Joyū hen, Danyū hen,* and *Kantoku hen*)
Tokyo: Kinema Junpōsha, 1995-1997.
『日本映画人名事典』(女優篇、男優篇、監督篇)キネマ旬報社, 1995-1997.

The core of this 5-volume name dictionary is built on the 1979-1980 *Nihon eiga haiyū zenshū* (1979-1980) and the *Nihon eiga, terebi kantoku zenshū,* which itself was based on the even earlier *Nihon eiga kantoku zenshū* (see both below). The *KineJun* actor/actress dictionaries vary less than the director dictionaries, but since the entry writers differ, it is still good to check both editions. The latest edition is by far the most impressive name dictionary out there. It includes both the famous and the obscure in equal measure. The set includes 1,385 directors (including young independents in their twenties), 2,035 actresses, and 1,952 actors. What makes this particularly impressive is the method of compilation. Drawing on its prestige and industry contacts, Kinema Junpōsha actually contacted everyone (at least if they were still living) and asked them to fill out a survey. These were then rewritten by an editorial staff that includes a number of very smart critics. This editorial process makes the *Nihon eiga jinmei jiten* the most trustworthy—though not infallible—source for biographical information, especially the proper pronunciation of names.

Nihon eiga kantoku zenshū
Tokyo: Kinema Junpōsha, 1976.
『日本映画監督全集』キネマ旬報社、1976.
Nihon eiga terebi kantoku zenshū = The directors
Tokyo: Kinema Junpōsha, 1988.
『日本映画テレビ監督全集 = The directors』キネマ旬報社、1988.

The 1990s Kinema Junpōsha director dictionary may be the most up-to-date book available (even though it is now already over a decade old), but these even older versions are worth a look themselves because they include different people, different text produced by different writers, and sometimes different information. For instance, the first one is best for early directors and can include quite detailed biographies by old authorities like Kishi Matsuo who personally knew these men. The second quite peculiarly divides living from dead directors, but offers sometimes insightful critical commentaries by major critics for the former (they can provide a succinct statement of what defines this auteur, which can be a good place to start thinking about these people). Libraries—and scholars—should try to own all three editions.

Nihon no eigajin: Nihon eiga no sōzōshatachi, edited by Satō Tadao
Tokyo: Nichigai Asoshiētsu, 2007.
佐藤忠男編『日本の映画人 日本映画の創造者たち』日外アソシエーツ: 発売元紀伊國屋書店, 2007.

This supersedes *Eizō media sakka jinmei jiten* with even more broad-reaching coverage of 1,472 personnel other than just actors and directors, including distributors, sound recordists, critics, scholars, composers, cinematographers, producers, studios, video artists, *benshi*, subtitlers, and festival programmers. Curiously, it also includes the results of questionnaires sent out to those still living about their personal interests.

Satsueijin meikan, edited by the J.S.C. Satsueijin Meikan Henshū Iinkai
Tokyo: Nihon Eiga Satsuei Kantoku Kyōkai, 2005.
J.S.C.撮影人名鑑編集委員会編『撮影人名鑑』日本映画撮影監督協会, 2005.

This lists the biographical data and contact information, main credits and awards for Japanese cinematographers—at least the members of the Japan Society of Cinematographers. Although it is meant to be something like a directory, there are curious sections for dead members and pioneers like Henry Kotani and Shibata Tsunekichi (but no addresses!). A fascinating chart in back traces the lineages of cameramen across time and by studio.

Tarento meiboroku
Tokyo: Rengō Tsūshinsha, 1965-.
『タレント名簿録』連合通信社, 1965-.

Otherwise known as "the Red Book," this is the red-covered companion to the *Geinōkai shinshiroku* (103). It lists currently available talent and their contact information, and is the best way to find the current contact information for actors and singers in the film, television and recording industries.

Terebi, tarento jinmei jiten
Tokyo: Nichigai Asoshiētsu, 2004.
『テレビ・タレント人名事典』日外アソシエーツ: 発売元 紀伊國屋書店, 2004.

A good guide to TV personalities, who can also frequently appear in films, especially now that the television networks have become more involved in film production. However, yearly guides to "*tarento*," such as the *Tarento meiboroku* (see above) or even those by *TV Guide*, can be more up-to-date for what is a very mercurial industry.

The Rest

The Benshi: Japanese Silent Film Narrators
Tokyo: Urban Connections, 2001.

Most of this small book is taken up by some thin history of the *benshi*, descriptions of major silent film theaters, and the somewhat mysterious inclusion of film synopses. It does, however, provide biographies of 27 well-known *benshi*.

Eiga sutā zenshū
Tokyo: Heibonsha, 1919-1930.
『映画スター全集』平凡社, 1919-1930.

This is a 10-volume biographical dictionary from the silent era. Each volume features four or five actors. The first two-thirds of a given book is filled with delicious photographs. Then each switches to biographies, some of which are autobiographical. This was aimed at fans of the day, not researchers in the future, so the writing is delightful. Reprinted in 2000 by Hon no Tomosha, so it's readily available.

Geinō jinbutsu jiten: Meiji, Taishō, Shōwa
Tokyo: Nichigai Asoshiētsu, 1998.

『芸能人物辞典　明治、大正、昭和』日外アソシエーツ, 1998.

This derivative name dictionary has very poor coverage, and is hardly worth a glance.

Kindai Nihon shakai undōshi jinbutsu daijiten, edited by Kindai Nihon Shakai Undōshi Jinbutsu Daijiten Henshū Iinkai
Tokyo: Nichigai Asoshiētsu, 1997.
近代日本社会運動史人物大事典編集委員会編『近代日本社会運動史人物大事典』日外アソシエーツ, 1997.

Marxism has been a strong force within the Japanese film world since the 1920s. This dictionary has profiles on all the major, and many of the minor, filmmakers and producers from the left. One can find biographical information on important writers like Atsugi Taka, Ueno Kōzō, Kanō Ryūichi and many others. Even for famous figures like Kurosawa Akira or Imai Tadashi, it can be interesting to see a career profile written from this particular point of view. Unfortunately, the selection is thoroughly oriented toward the prewar period.

Nihon dokyumentarī eiga zenshi, by Noda Shinkichi
Tokyo: Shakai Shisōsha, 1984.
野田真吉著『日本ドキュメンタリー映画全史』社会思想社, 1984.

Although billed as the "complete history of Japanese documentary," this short book by one of the movers and shakers in postwar documentary is more like a biographical dictionary of Japanese nonfiction filmmakers.

Nihon geinō jinmei jiten, edited by Kurata Yoshihiro and Fujinami Takayuki
Tokyo: Sanseidō, 1995.
倉田喜弘, 藤波隆之編『日本芸能人名事典』三省堂, 1995.

Extremely short entries, especially for postwar actors, and thus of little use.

Nihon musei eiga haiyū meikan/The Great Japanese Silent Movie Stars, edited by Musei Eiga Kanshōkai
Tokyo: Urban Connections, 2005.
無声映画鑑賞会編『日本無声映画俳優名鑑』アーバン・コネクションズ, 2005.

This is another project from Matsuda Film Productions (17-18). It was produced in conjunction with Urban Connections, a translation company whose CEO, Larry Greenberg, is a silent film fan. Filmographies are partial and pickings are slim (even at 175 names), but it's a significant resource in English. Their selection of actors was based on a silent era *banzuke* and a 1970s poll. The book is profusely illustrated, so anyone wondering what's for sale in the Matsuda Film Productions collection can use this as a starting point.

Seiyū jiten
Tokyo: Kinema Junpōsha, 1994.
『声優事典』キネマ旬報社, 1994.

Identical to *Seiyu meikan* (below), except half the entries. So why bother?

Seiyū meikan
Tokyo: Seibidō Shuppan, 1999.
『声優名鑑』成美堂出版, 1999.

Voice actors in Japan enjoy a vigorous and slightly bizarre star system, and this book evinces the power of their aural aura. Well over 700 pages, it lists 1,027 women and 870 men with *rubi* transliterations of their names. The data includes a profile, date-of-birth, birthplace, original name, all graced with a face shot. The back has a set of unusual chronologies for release and start dates for animated films, television series, OVAs, and voice actor CDs.

Chronologies

Japanese authors love nenpyō, *or chronological timelines. It's such a strong convention in publishing that it's typical to find timelines in the back of books and catalogs, but no index. We would take the latter over the former any day. However, timelines do have their place, especially at the beginning of a project when one wants to get a feel for the general landscape of a given moment or period in film history. Here are five good ones.*

Eiga hyakunen: Eiga wa kō shite hajimatta, edited by Yomiuri Shinbun Bunkabu
Tokyo: Kinema Junpōsha, 1997.
読売新聞文化部編『映画百年　映画はこうして始まった』キネマ旬報社, 1997.

The first half of this cinema centenary book is a trivial collection of two-page articles, but the second half is a long timeline of Japanese cinema. This is less complex than the ones below, but more linear and focused on the film world. There are indexes for names and titles.

Nenpyō eiga 100-nenshi, by Tanikawa Yoshio
Tokyo: Fūtōsha, 1993.
谷川義男『年表・映画100年史』風濤社, 1993.

For someone looking for an instant snap-shot of a particular year in film, this might be the first place to look. Tanikawa loves listing, and this book-length timeline bears the mark of his personality. Boxes for every year note major films, awards, incidents—all laid against larger historical events. Comes with a handy name index.

Nihon eiga hattatsushi, by Tanaka Jun'ichirō
Tokyo: Chūō Kōronsha, 1980.
田中純一郎『日本映画発達史』中央公論社, 1980.

The last volume of Tanaka's massive history has a timeline that is indexed to the history written in the first four.

Nihon eigashi, zōhoban, by Satō Tadao
Tokyo: Iwanami Shoten, 2006-2007.
佐藤忠男著『日本映画史』増補版, 岩波書店, 2006-2007.

The fourth volume of Satō's canonical history is largely taken up by a long chronology of Japanese film.

Nihon eigashi taikan: Eiga torai kara gendai made 86-nenkan no kiroku, by Matsuura Kōzō
Tokyo: Bunka Shuppankyoku, 1982.
松浦幸三編著『日本映画史大鑑・映画渡来から現代まで・86年間の記録』文化出版局, 1982.

This chronology is perhaps the best one could hope for. Over the course of his life, Matsuura was an editor for publications like *Makino purodakushon*, *Eiga fan*, and *Kindai eiga*. He probably spent his entire career immersed in the details of the feature film world; at least this is the impression one gets from reading his chronology. There is a density to the entries that allows the reader to leave the text with a sense for the complexity of film history—its gossip, celebrations, tragedies, publishing activities, and constantly shifting industrial structures. Worth a read by any serious student of Japanese film. Covers the beginning of film to 1982.

Script Collections and Collected Works of Directors

Many great authors in Japan are celebrated through publication of their collected or complete works. Few individuals in the film world have enjoyed such status. Imamura Taihei is about the only critic to be so honored (see p. 78), and only a small number of directors or screenwriters have been the subject of multi-volume collections. Those researching the breadth of discourse on film should note that, since many novelists and thinkers wrote on film in Japan, their collected or complete works can also contain a significant volume of cinema-related writing. Figures we do not list here include Gonda Yasunosuke, Nakai Masakazu, Naoki Sanjūgo, Inagaki Taruho, Tanizaki Jun'ichirō, Terada Torahiko, Haniya Yutaka, Haneda Kiyoteru, Tsurumi Shunsuke, Abe Kōbō, Takeda Taijun, Mishima Yukio, and others.

One fortunate aspect of the Japanese film world—though one that ironically underlines how much the word is valued more than the image in official culture—is that scripts and screenwriting have been highly respected. That is why there are numerous collections of printed screenplays. In this section, we introduce some of the major multi-volume collections of screenplays, especially ones centered on a particular screenwriter or director (note that such collections can also include other kinds of writing by that person). There are many single-volume collections that we do not list here, but if a library does possess the following, it has a solid collection for researching screenplays.

Screenplays can be useful not only when studying screenwriting or the production of an individual film, but also when a film print is not subtitled and you cannot pick up all the dialogue. The scenario can help you follow the film, but one should note that the art of "scenario literature" is so honored in Japan, that many publications prefer to print the script as it was originally written, not as it was eventually filmed. Such discrepancies, however, can be interesting in themselves as indications of the creative process pursued by directors or other personnel on the set.

The Best of the Best

Shinario bunken, by Tanikawa Yoshio
Tokyo: Fūtōsha, 1984.
谷川義雄編『シナリオ文献』風濤社, 1997.

Tanikawa Yoshio's *Shinario bunken* is the only decent index to published film scripts, including those printed in major magazines such as *Shinario* or *Kinema junpō* and in anthologies like *Nenkan daihyō shinarioshū*. The index is culled from nearly 60 journals and 80 scenario collections, and reaches back to the 1920s. Originally published in 1979, it was updated in 1984 and 1997 (each contains an errata sheet that often goes missing). If you cannot find a script here, you probably have to go to Waseda University's Tsubouchi Memorial Theatre Museum (28-29), where they have their own in-house card-based index. Another resource is Kawakita's online database (12-13), which can allow you to search the table of contents of books.

The Best

Hito to shinario
Tokyo: Shinario Sakka Kyōkai, 1989-.
『人とシナリオ』シナリオ作家協会, 1989-.

A series of single volumes (twelve so far) each focusing on a famous scriptwriter published by the Association of Scenario Writers Japan. It includes screenwriters like Ide Masato, Hashimoto Shinobu, Suzuki Naoyuki, Yamanouchi Hisashi, Yasumi Toshio and Tamura Tsutomu.

Itami Mansaku zenshū
Tokyo: Chikuma Shobō, 1961.
『伊丹万作全集』筑摩書房, 1961.

A collection of not only some of the scripts, but also much of the critical writing of Itami Mansaku, the father of Jūzō and one of the great prewar directors and thinkers.

Itō Daisuke shinario shū
Kyoto-shi: Tankōsha, 1985.
『伊藤大輔シナリオ集』淡交社, 1985.

A four-volume collection of Itō Daisuke's scripts, from the silent *jidaigeki* masterpieces he directed to postwar works written for others. Many of Itō's personal copies, filled with annotations, are preserved at the Museum of Kyoto (18-19).

Kikushima Ryūzō shinario senshū
Tokyo: Sanreniti: Seiunsha, 1984.
『菊島隆三シナリオ選集』サンレニティ: 星雲社, 1984.

A three-volume collection of the screenplays of Kikushima Ryūzō, one of Japan's most prominent screenwriters who worked with Kurosawa Akira, Masumura Yasuzō, Inagaki Hiroshi, Shibuya Minoru, Naruse Mikio, Kawashima Yuzō, and Imai Tadashi, among others.

Nakajima Takehiro shinario senshū
Tokyo: Eijinsha, 2003.
『中島丈博シナリオ選集』映人社, 2003.

A three-volume collection of the man who wrote the scripts for such films as *Tsugaru jongara bushi, Matsuri no junbi, A haru,* and *Okoge* (which he also directed).

Nenkan daihyō shinarioshū
Tokyo: Eijinsha.
『年鑑代表シナリオ集』映人社.

A yearly anthology of the ten or so "best" screenplays from that year, selected by the Association of Scenario Writers Japan. The series began with a volume covering 1945-1951 and continues to this day. In terms of sheer volume, this is the richest collection of scripts in book form.

Nihon shinario bungaku zenshū
Tokyo: Rironsha, 1955-1956.
『日本シナリオ文学全集』理論社, 1955-1956.
A collection of scripts divided into twelve *shinsho*-sized volumes, with most dedicated to one author. Many of the scripts found here of big names like Ozu, Kurosawa, Yamanaka, and Itami Mansaku are covered in other collections, but there are also volumes dedicated to Mizuki Yōko, Hisaita Eijirō, Yagi Yasutarō, Shiina Rinzō, and Abe Kōbō.

Nihon shinario taikei, edited by Shinario Sakka Kyōkai
Tokyo: Maruyon Shinario Bunko, 1973-1979.
シナリオ作家協会編纂『日本シナリオ大系』マリヨンシナリオ文庫, 1973-1979.

In six volumes, this is the major anthology of classic and canonical screenplays, featuring works from the silent era up until the 1970s. Every research library should have it.

Nihon eiga shinario koten zenshū
Tokyo: Kinema Junpōsha, 1965-1966.
『日本映画シナリオ古典全集』キネマ旬報社, 1965-66.
Nihon eiga daihyō shinario zenshū
Tokyo: Kinema Junpōsha, 1957-.
『日本映画代表シナリオ全集』キネマ旬報社, 1957-.

These two six-volume script collections by *KineJun* were printed simply as special issues of the magazine and thus are not as physically sturdy as the *Shinario taikei*. They also focus exclusively on prewar and wartime films. But they are two of the major collections beyond the *Shinario taikei* and while a lot of films are duplicated between the three collections, there are some significant differences.

Otoko wa tsurai yo, by Yamada Yōji
Tokyo: Rippū Shobō, 1976.
山田洋次著『男はつらいよ』立風書房, 1976.

A nine-volume, *bunko*-size collection of scripts for the *Otoko wa tsurai yo* or Tora-san series, covering the first 27 films. This supercedes an earlier four-volume collection.

Ozu Yasujirō zenshū
Tokyo: Shinshokan, 2003.
井上和男編『小津安二郎全集』新書館, 2003.

A three-volume collection of the scripts of many of Ozu's films. It also contains scripts that Ozu penned for other directors.

Sekai no eiga sakka
Tokyo: Kinema Junpōsha, 1970-1980.
『世界の映画作家』キネマ旬報社, 1970-1980.

This ambitious project by *KineJun* produced forty volumes dedicated to a variety of subjects, mostly auteur studies, but also national film histories and genre studies. Seven of the volumes focus on Japanese directors, some two a volume, including directors often overlooked in the West like Saitō Kōichi, Katō Tai, Kumashiro Tatsumi, Urayama Kirirō, and Kumai Kei. In addition to critical commentaries and interviews, the scripts of one or two films are printed for each director.

Shinario
Tokyo: Shinario Sakka Kyōkai.
『シナリオ』シナリオ作家協会.

Begun in 1946, *Shinario* is the most important and longest-running screenwriting journal. It usually publishes two to three scripts of films in current release with each monthly issue. It also includes director interviews and articles by screenwriters.

Shindō Kaneto no eiga chosakushū
Komae-chō, Tokyo: Pōrie Kikaku, 1970-.

『新藤兼人の映画著作集』ポーリエ企画, 1970-.

A four-volume collection of screenplays as well as the writings of Shindō Kaneto, famous not only as a director and screenwriter, but also as a prolific writer on cinema and society. There are other single-volume collections of his screenplays.

Yamada Yōji sakuhinshū, by Yamada Yōji
Tokyo: Rippū Shobō, 1979-1980.
山田洋次『山田洋次作品集』立風書房, 1979-1980.

An eight-volume collection that also contains scripts for some of the *Otoko wa tsurai yo* films, but focuses mostly on Yamada's other works.

Yamanaka Sadao sakuhinshū
Tokyo: Jitsugyō no Nihonsha, 1985-1986.
『山中貞雄作品集』実業之日本社, 1985-1986.

A collection of scripts in three volumes, plus a *bekkan*. Since only three of the films of this brilliant director, who tragically died at the age of 29, remain today in largely complete form, these scripts are one of the few means of accessing his larger oeuvre. The collection was re-edited and compressed into one thick tome by the same publisher in 1998. It also put out a companion volume, *Kantoku Yamanaka Sadao* (edited by Chiba Nobuo), that amasses all the pre-war writings on Yamanaka. Some of Yamanaka's personal scripts are held by the Museum of Kyoto (18-19).

Zenshū Kurosawa Akira
Tokyo: Iwanami Shoten, 1987-1988.
『全集黒沢明』岩波書店, 1987-1988.

A six-volume collection of all of Kurosawa's scripts—including ones he did not direct—up until *Ran*.

Censorship

Censorship records can be helpful in determining if a film was cut by the censors, and if so, what was changed. Since almost all films made after 1925, when censorship was nationalized, until the end of the war, were required to undergo censorship screening, censorship records can provide some of the best data on what films were made, who made them, how many prints were struck (since it was prints that were censored, not films), their length, and the category of film. This can be extremely helpful for researching minor works not found in the usual filmographies.

For research into primary materials, there are two massive collections that are fully accessible and fairly well indexed: the Prange Collection (10-12) and the U.S. National Archives (19-21). The National Diet Library in Tokyo (21-23) has the bulk of both censorship collections on microfilm.

The Best

Katsudō shashin firumu ken'etsu jihō, by Naimushō Keihokyoku
Tokyo: Fuji Shuppan, 1985-1986.
内務省警保局『活動寫眞フヰルム検閲時報』不二出版, 1985-1986.
Eiga ken'etsu jihō, by Naimushō Keihokyoku
Tokyo: Fuji Shuppan, 1986.
内務省警保局『映画検閲時報』不二出版, 1986.

A reprint of the in-house bulletins that the Ministry of Home Affairs published to report on its film censorship activities. The first series covers the years 1925 to 1939 and the second 1939 to 1943. The title changed as censorship procedures were altered with the institution of the Film Law in 1939, but the primary aim for both is to list all the films that were censored and detail whatever changes were made. The publications also include ministry directives. They are clumsy to use: if you know the release date of a film, you have to check the bulletins printed around that time and just pore over the lists. There is no order other than censorship number. Every film print should have been censored so the initial list can serve as the best record of what was made, by whom, and how long the print was. If the main list notes the film had suffered cuts or other censorship action, you can check the appendix for a description of the changes ordered.

Nihon eiga ken'etsushi, by Makino Mamoru
Tokyo: Pandora/Gendai Shokan, 2003.
牧野守著『日本映画検閲史』パンドラ: 発売 現代書館, 2003.

Reprinting unusual materials is a writing strategy in Makino Mamoru's 700-page opus on censorship to 1945, the most important work on government film policy regulation so far. In addition to the extensive and lengthy quotes embedded in the author's analysis, all the major regulations and laws from the period are reprinted in the back. Thus while the book is occasionally short on analysis, it is a fount of information that we should be thankful finally got published. Given the lack of support for serious research in film history in either academia or publishing, it took decades for this to finally hit the market.

Photos, Posters, Programs

*Especially since film is largely a visual medium, there are many times when the researcher wishes to reference visual, not linguistic data. Beyond, of course, the film itself, stills, posters, star photos, programs, handbills (*chirashi*) and other materials with a strong visual component are needed either for analysis or for use in presentations or publications. A dictionary or database of stills has yet to be produced, however. Fortunately, there are a number of published resources for obtaining such materials. Stills and posters are relatively easy: beyond finding them in books devoted to the film or director, they can be found in works concentrating on reproducing visual material related to a certain topic. Waizu Shuppan, for instance, has been printing dozens of books in the last decade, mostly individually but some in series, that reproduce stills and posters in large numbers about various genres and performers. Some books publishing handbills, still a major form of film advertising as the lobby of most any Japanese theater has piles of them, have also come out. Another source is film programs.*

One peculiarity of Japanese film culture is the continued popularity of theater programs, which are basically pamphlets produced on the film that are sold at the theater. In the early years, the theaters themselves produced the program and distributed it for free, but they are now made by the distributor and sold at cinemas around the country. Programs can be a good source not only for stills, but also for credits, advertising discourse (how the film was sold), and even interviews, commentary and sometimes the script. The Film Center, Waseda, and the Ōtani Library all have significant collections, and in North America, Columbia has programs in the Makino Collection and Yale is currently building up a collection. Some older pamphlets have been collected and reproduced in book form, however, for instance in a few local histories. Here we introduce in alphabetical order some of the major largely multi-volume collections of Japanese-film-related visual materials like posters, stills and pamphlets.

Anime chirashi dai-katarogu: Hōgaban, edited by Yoshida Yōichi
Tokyo: Keibunsha, 2000.
吉田陽一 編『アニメチラシ大カタログ　邦画版』勁文社, 2000.

Features not just anime handbills, but also posters, pamphlets, press sheets, and tickets.

Minishiatā furaiyā korekushon
Tokyo: Pie Books, 2004-2007.
『ミニシアターフライヤーコレクション』Pie Books, 2004-2007.

Minishiatā gurafikkusu
Tokyo: Pie Books, 2003-2007.
『ミニシアターグラフィックス』Pie Books, 2003-2007.

Both of these two-volume collections are centered on the visual design strategies contemporary mini-theaters have used to promote their films, Japanese or foreign. The stress is on cute and fashionable design, with plenty of examples of handbills, cards, pamphlets and other advertising material.

Natsukashi no Nihon eiga posutā korekushon
Tokyo: Kindai Eigasha, 1989-1990.
『なつかしの日本映画ポスターコレクション』近代映画社, 1989-1990.

A two-volume collection of posters mostly centered on the 1950s and 1960s with the first book featuring classic works such as those by Ozu or Kurosawa, and the second movies of popular stars such as Ichikawa Raizō, Misora Hibari, Hasegawa Kazuo or Katsu Shintarō.

Nihon eiga posutā shū
Tokyo: Waizu Shuppan, 2000-2003.
『日本映画ポスター集』ワイズ出版, 2000-2003.

A non-numbered series of volumes devoted to film posters, divided by studio, genre and theme. Given that the publisher is Waizu Shuppan and that many of the tomes are edited by Maruo Toshirō, most are devoted to popular cinema, especially of the action or *eroguro* kind. There are thus volumes on Shin Tōhō, Daini Tōei, Roman Poruno, pink film, *femmes fatale*, and Nikkatsu Action, although there are also books on Nikkatsu youth film and avant garde works.

Nihon eiga sengo ōgon jidai, edited by Sengo Nihon Eiga Kenkyūkai
Tokyo: Nihon Bukku Raiburarī, 1978.
戦後日本映画研究会編集『日本映画戦後黄金時代』日本ブックライブラリー, 1978.

Basically a 30-volume collection of stills, with each volume devoted to a studio, period or genre. With each book including an essay on the subject of the volume, the series also provides a decent overview of postwar cinema.

Nihon eiga suchīru shū
Tokyo: Waizu Shuppan, 2001-2002.
『日本映画スチール集』ワイズ出版, 2001-2002.

Another non-numbered series from Waizu Shuppan focusing this time on stills. Again divided by studio, genre and theme, the volumes focus on popular cinema, especially B-movie *jidaigeki*. Most of the series entries were edited by Ishiwari Osamu and Maruo Toshirō.

21-seiki eiga chirashi korekushon 2000-2004
Tokyo: Kinema Junpōsha, 2006.
『21世紀映画チラシコレクション 2000-2004』キネマ旬報社, 2006.

A valuable book for anyone who is not just looking for the *chirashi* for a single film, but studying the contemporary phenomenon of movie handbills. This reproduces the *chirashi* of about 2,250 Japanese and foreign films released between 2000 and 2004, and in some cases, includes variant editions, such as ones made for different localities, for special tie-ups, or other reasons.

Omoide no puroguramu: Shinkyōgoku hen, edited by Tanaka Yasuhiko
Kyoto: Kyō o Kataru Kai, 1980.
田中泰彦編集・解説『思い出のプログラム　新京極篇』京を語る会, 1980.

A volume that reproduces programs from the main theaters in Kyoto's Shinkyōgoku, the main movie theater district in the old capital, dating from the late Meiji to the end of WWII.

Puroguramu eigashi: Taishō kara senchū made: natsukashi no fukkoku-ban, edited by Nihon Eiga Terebi Purodyūsā Kyōkai
Tokyo: Nihon Hōsō Shuppan Kyōkai, 1978.
日本映画テレビプロデューサー協会編『プログラム映画史　大正から戦中まで懐しの復刻版』日本放送出版協会, 1978.

A well-done, two-volume collection of film theater programs from the 1920s up until the wartime.

Ryūkōka to eiga de miru Shōwa jidai, edited by Endō Noriaki with introductions by Ashihara Kuniko
Tokyo: Kokusho Kankōkai, 1986.
遠藤憲昭編, 葦原邦子解説『流行歌と映画でみる昭和時代』国書刊行会, 1986.
Ryūkōka to eiga de miru sengo jidai, edited by Endō Noriaki
Tokyo: Kokusho Kankōkai, 1986.
遠藤憲昭編『流行歌と映画でみる戦後時代』国書刊行会, 1986.

These two, two-volume sets cover film and popular song up before and after 1945.

Shashinshū eiga ōgonki koya to meisaku no fūkei
Tokyo: Kokusho Kankōkai, 1989.
『写真集映画黄金期・小屋と名作の風景』国書刊行会, 1989.

A two-volume collection of old photos of theaters from around the country.

Shashin kaiga shūsei Nihon eiga no rekishi, edited by Iwamoto Kenji
Tokyo: Nihon Tosho Sentā, 1998.
岩本憲児編著『写真・絵画集成　日本映画の歴史』日本図書センター, 1998.

This attractive, 3-volume collection of mostly black and white stills and photos attempts to visually present film history in a more comprehensive fashion, covering not just stills and star portraits, but photos of theaters, theater districts, technology, and other related items.

Teito fūgirikan: Senzen eiga puroguramu korekushon, edited by Matsuda Shū
Tokyo: Firumu Ātosha, 1994.
松田集 編集『帝都封切館　戦前映画プログラムコレクション』フィルムアート社, 1994.

Focuses on prewar programs of foreign film theaters.

Film Periodicals

Film magazines and journals are not necessarily reference sources, but some like Kinema junpō, *as we have seen, devote considerable energy to establishing an authoritative record of the film industry and its products. This is one reason for including periodicals in this bibliography. But another reason is simpler: the study of cinema was ignored for so long in Japan and the United States that few institutions put much effort into collecting film-related journals and magazines. The result is that even major libraries do not have complete runs of the important Japanese journals and lesser-known—but still important—periodicals are hard to find. Locating journals can be a task itself even when one knows what one is looking for, and with few periodical indexes covering film magazines, it is hard to learn what to look for in the first place. The Makino (81) and the Takarazuka (84) indexes are a (hard-to-use) start for the prewar, but the* Zasshi kiji sakuin *for a long time ignored the majority of film magazines (*KineJun *was not indexed before the 1970s and* Eiga geijutsu *was omitted). The situation has improved. Reprints of old journals have not only made them more available but, with some including indexes, easier to use. You can now find earlier postwar* *articles indexed in online databases like Magazine Plus. But there are still many gaps and smaller journals are not yet included. Also, indexing is still imprecise so smaller articles—like film reviews—often do not show up in the database.*

The long and short of it then is that it is still important for scholars to find and physically leaf through a film journal to obtain articles for research. That means knowing which journals to look at and where to find them is a crucial skill. With few film magazines being reproduced through microfilm or electronic means, there are still dozens of important journals that can only be accessed through their original physical form. We thus felt it important to direct researchers on where to start.

Here are some of the most important Japanese film periodicals in terms of their depth of content, their place in the history of film criticism or journalism, and their influence. We want to emphasize that this is only a gesture to the richest and historically important journals; there are literally hundreds of others. If one includes the newsletters of industry groups, studios, theaters, fans, unions and other organizations, the numbers of periodicals for Japanese cinema surely tops 1,000.

The Big Three

Eiga geijutsu = Quarterly eigageijutsu (1946-)
『映画芸術 = Quarterly eiga geijutsu』

Published on and off since 1946, *Eigei* was one of the big three postwar magazines alongside *KineJun* and *Eiga hyōron,* but with the latter ceasing publication, it is now just *KineJun* and *Eigei.* This was a monthly run by Ogawa Tōru in the 1960s, who especially promoted writing by artists outside film. The magazine eventually shifted to quarterly publication and is now edited by the screenwriter Arai Haruhiko with a quirky, more independent perspective than *KineJun.*

Eiga hyōron (1926-1975)
『映画評論』

One of the big three film magazines in Japan, *Eiga hyōron's* history can be traced back to 1926, with some changes during and after the war. Always focused more on film criticism than *KineJun,* which was also a trade journal, the magazine enjoyed as editors famous critics like Satō Tadao and Satō Shigeomi. Especially under the latter's direction, the magazine championed underground cinema and denigrated genres like yakuza and pink film. Ended publication in 1975.

Kinema junpō (1919-)
『キネマ旬報』
Kinema junpō = The movie times

Tokyo: Yūshōdō Shuppan, 1993-1995.
『キネマ旬報 = The movie times.』雄松堂出版, 1993-1995.
Eiga junpō
Tokyo: Yumani Shobō, 2004.
『映画旬報』ゆまに書房, 2004.
Kinema junpō = The movie times
Tokyo: Bunsei Shoin, 2009.
『キネマ旬報 = The movie times.』文生書院, 2009.

Kinema junpō is the most important film journal in Japan, concentrating on film criticism and trade news. It started as a coterie publication in 1919 and lasted until 1941 when the government forced it to change its *katakana* title to *Eiga junpō*. There was a fitful attempt to restart it after the war, but publication only resumed for good after 1950. Since *KineJun* made an effort to print not only reviews, but also *"shōkai"* (basically credits and plot summary) of every commercial film released in Japan, it is an essential source for beginning to research a film. Many of the major critics wrote for it and the industry analysis is also important, although its stance has been relatively conservative and a target of criticism for other journals trying to distinguish themselves. The second issue in February (the February 15 issue or *"gejungō"*) is the Best Ten issue, featuring both the results of the *Kinema junpō* Best Ten, the critics poll that has become the longest running film award in Japan, and a detailed overview of the industry in the previous year. Unfortunately, no institution outside of Japan has a complete run of this journal. However, thanks to the reprints by Yūshōdō, Bunsei Shoin and Yumani, the prewar volumes and the entire run of *Eiga junpō* are widely available.

Early Journals

Katsudō shashinkai (1909-1911)
Tokyo: Kokusho Kankōkai, 1999.
『活動寫眞界』国書刊行会, 1999.

A reprint of one of the first film magazines. Associated with Yoshizawa Shōten, it was a high-class journal featuring submissions by many illuminati. Originally published by Nihon Katsudōsha from 1909 to 1911.

Kinema rekōdō = Kinema-record (1913-1917)
Tokyo: Kokusho Kankōkai, 1999-2000.
『キネマ・レコード = Kinema-record』国書刊行会, 1999-2000.

A reprint of the journal, mostly edited by Shigeno Yukiyoshi and Kaeriyama

Norimasa, that was central in the movement for reform in Japanese cinema. While calling for the creation of "pure films," the journal also promoted film criticism and prided itself for being a trade journal, offering close analysis of technical and business practices in the industry. It began publication in October 1913 under the title *Firumu rekōdo*, but changed to *Kinema rekōdo* with the fifth issue in December. Originally published semimonthly (Oct. 1913-Feb. 1914), and monthly (Mar. 1914-July 1917): Tokyo: Firumu Rekōdosha, 1913: Kinema Rekōdosha, 1914-July 1917: Kinogurafusha, Oct. 1917-Dec. 1917.

Nihon eiga shoki shiryō shūsei
Tokyo: San'ichi Shōbō, 1990-1991.
『日本映画初期資料集成』三一書房, 1990-1991.
[1-2] *Katsudō shashin zasshi* (1915). -- [3-5] *Katsudō no sekai* (1916). -- [6-9] *Katsudō gahō* (1917).

This compilation reprints the first year or so of three early film magazines. *Katsudō shashin zasshi* was a more popular-oriented magazine begun in 1915; *Katsudō no sekai*, started in 1916, was nearly as reformist as *Kinema rekōdo;* and *Katsudō gahō* was another popular, but more visually oriented publication begun in 1917. The three together offer a good slice of late 1910s film culture.

Left-Leaning Periodicals

Eiga hihyō (1970-1973)
『映画批評』

This monthly magazine founded by Matsuda Masao and published by Shinsensha was the center of New Left film writings in the early 1970s with contributors such as Adachi Masao, Hiraoka Masaaki, and Sasaki Mamoru.

Eiga sōzō (1936-1937)
Tokyo: Fuji Shuppan, 1986.
『映畫創造』不二出版, 1986.

Reprint of an important left-wing theoretical journal from the late 1930s. It featured writers like Tosaka Jun, Iwasaki Akira, Imamura Taihei, and Ueno Kōzō.

Prewar Proletarian Film Movement Reprint Series
Ann Arbor, MI: University of Michigan Center for Japanese Studies Publications Program, 2004.

[1] *Eiga no eiga* (1927-28). -- [2] *Eiga kaihō* (1928). -- [3] *Eichō* (1925-1930). -- [4] *Eiga kōjō* (1927-1928). -- [5] *Eiga dōkōkai* (1932). -- [6] *Eiga totsugekitai* (1930-1933). -- [7] *Nihon eiga rōdō nenpō* (1933-1934). -- [8] *Shinkō eiga* (1929-1930). -- [9] *Puroretaria eiga* (1928). -- [10] *Purokino* (1932). -- [11] *Dai niji puroretaria eiga* (1930-1931). -- [12] *Eiga kurabu* (1932-1933).

This online reprint series was edited by Makino Mamoru and Markus, drawing on treasures from the deep nooks and crannies of the Makino Collection (8-9). While a handful of the journals were beautifully reproduced on paper in the Senki Fukkokuban Kankōkai series (below), this project provides easier access and a crucial historiographic correction. The paper reprint, which Makino was also involved in, was the project of former members of the Proletarian Film League of Japan (or Prokino). In a final snub of their prewar competitors, the Senki Sukkokuban Kankōkai excluded publications by the Puroretaria Eiga Renmei and other independent groups.

Each issue can be read page by page in a viewer, or downloaded in its entirety as a pdf file. Covers and color plates may be examined in a separate image database. It is missing a few numbers, but it is online and free. Unfortunately, it is not searchable, but the *bekkan* for the *Shōwa shoki sayoku eiga zasshi* contains an index for many of the Prokino-produced journals (below). The site is accompanied by a number of books and Prokino films in quicktime. There is also a small collection of records from the censorship office. Aside from their obvious value as research material on censorship, these newsletters and pamphlets give a sense for the minor left-wing literature that is lost to history.

Shine furonto (1976-)
『シネ・フロント』

First published by the Eiga Kanshō Dantai Zenkoku Renraku Kaigi, an organization associated with the Japanese Communist Party, and later by Shine Furonto-sha, *Shine furonto* has featured the writings of such left critics as Yamada Kazuo and Yoshimura Hideo, and championed social problem films and the works of Yamada Yōji and Shindō Kaneto.

Shōwa shoki sayoku eiga zasshi
Tokyo: Senki Fukkokuban Kankōkai, 1981.
『昭和初期左翼映画雑誌』戦旗復刻版刊行会, 1981.
[1] *Shinkō eiga* (1929-1930). -- [2] *Puroretaria eiga* (1928). -- [3] *Purokino* (1932). -- [4] *Dai niji puroretaria eiga* (1930-1931). -- [5] *Eiga kurabu* (1932-1933).

The first attempt to preserve the heritage of Japanese film magazine through reprinting, this covers the important left-wing and proletarian film magazines published in early Shōwa. This is probably the most beautifully realized reprint for Japanese cinema. It faithfully reproduces the original color, size, and paper texture of each individual issue; what's more, each number is printed separately rather than bound by volume. It is also accompanied by several tickets and theater programs, and a stunning poster. Most of this reprint is now available through the University of Michigan Center for Japanese Studies Publications Program electronic reprint series (above). A *bekkan* has a complete index of the set.

Academic Journals

Eigagaku (1987-)
『映画学』

Begun in 1987, this is the annual publication of Waseda University's graduate program in film studies. Scholarly in nature, it contains many important articles, even if many are by grad students and thus still unpolished.

Eigashi kenkyū (1973-1990)
『映画史研究』

Personally edited and published by Satō Tadao and his wife Satō Hisako, this irregularly published periodical featured many precise, empirical articles on specific aspects of Japanese film history, including many more obscure topics, especially on early cinema, that other journals would not touch. There were even a few articles in English.

Eizōgaku (1975-)
『映像学』

Started in 1975 as *Kikan eizō,* this is the official journal of the Nihon Eizō Gakkai (Japan Society of Image Arts and Sciences), the main academic society that includes film studies. Although the society encompasses a variety of modern image media fields, the majority of articles in the journal have been on film. By default, in a sense, it is the primary academic film journal in Japan.

Industry Oriented

Kinema shūhō (1930-1939)
Tokyo: Yumani Shobō, 2008-.
『キネマ週報』

Kinema shūhō was established in 1930 as something of a reposte to Ichikawa Sai's *Kokusai eiga shinbun.* The founding editor was Tanaka Jun'ichirō, who handed off the reins to the unlikely combination of former censor Tachibana Takahiro and former Prokino member Sasa Genjū. It is invaluable for learning what was going on in the film business in the 1930s. It folded in 1939.

Kokusai eiga shinbun = The international motion picture news (1927-1937)
Tokyo: Yumani Shobō, 2005.
『國際映画新聞 = The International motion picture news』ゆまに書房, 2005.

A reprint of one of the most important prewar trade publications, edited by Ichikawa Sai from 1927 to 1937. Significantly, the final volume of the reprint contains an index of articles, a rare addition amongst the film periodical reprints.

Production Oriented

Eiga kagaku kenkyū (1928-1932)
『映画科学研究』

This journal reflects how many Japanese filmmakers have also been scholars of the medium. Edited by the *gendaigeki* directors Murata Minoru and Ushihara Kiyohiko, it was an effort by those in film production—with occasional articles by film critics—to methodically investigate and analyze various aspects of their medium, from scriptwriting and sound to editing (montage) and industrial structure. The thick issues would include scripts, translations of foreign articles, and even speculations about proletarian film. A total of ten issues were published.

Eiga terebi gijutsu (1948-)
『映画テレビ技術』

This is the official organ of the Motion Picture and Television Engineering Society of Japan. It is the domestic equivalent of the *SMPTE Journal,* although the Japanese version includes features and reports from the set. A complete index from 1944 to 2004 is available on their website (www.mpte.jp/html/mptebook/downsvc.html).

Shinario (1946-)
『シナリオ』

Shinario is the venerable screenwriting journal published by the writers' own union. It's also the oldest script magazine, having been established in 1946. A typical issue has several new scenarios, accompanied by features and interviews.

Popular Criticism

Eiga no tomo (1931-1968)
『映画之友』

This fan journal can trace its lineage back to 1924 and the magazine *Eiga sekai*, which was published by Tachibana Kōichirō's Eiga Sekaisha with help from Furukawa Roppa. Tachibana changed its name to *Eiga no tomo* in 1931 and, even after suffering forced mergers and stoppages during the war, revived the magazine in 1946. Its subsequent run as one of the top foreign film magazines was shaped by the editorship of Yodogawa Nagaharu, one of the most popular postwar critics, and the writings of such critics as Komori Shizuko. After the magazine stopped publication in 1968, another publisher, Kindai Eigasha, revived the name in the late seventies as an idol/nudie magazine.

Kindai eiga (1945-)
『近代映画』

First started as a fan magazine covering both Japanese and foreign film, *Kindai eiga* eventually became the main periodical in the 1950s and 1960s covering Japanese movies from a popular perspective. It became primarily an idol magazine in the 1970s and changed its title to *Kindai* in the late nineties. The same publisher, Kindai Eigasha, began publishing *Screen* in 1946, which has continued to be one of the top foreign movie fan magazines.

Nihon eiga (1936-1945)
Tokyo: Yumani Shobō, 2002-2003.
『日本映画』ゆまに書房, 2002-2003.

Originally published monthly by the Dai Nihon Eiga Kyōkai from 1936-1945. Since the Kyōkai was half a private, half a government institution, *Nihon eiga* has the strong tone of being the sole official film publication as Japan marched towards war. It was in fact the only one to last until nearly the end of the war. One achieves a sense of the march towards disaster in the format, which starts out with colorful covers and a thick heft to each issue; however, by the end of the war it was reduced to a thin trade newsletter circulating only within the industry.

Cineaste Oriented

Cahiers du cinéma Japon (1991-2001)

Started in 1991 with links to the French *Cahiers du cinéma*, *Cahiers Japan* was edited by Umemoto Yōichi and focused largely on foreign film. Influenced by Hasumi Shigehiko's critical writings, it also spotlighted Japanese directors close to him, such as Kurosawa Kiyoshi and Aoyama Shinji. The last issue in 2001 was devoted to Aoyama's *Eureka.*

Eiga geijutsu kenkyū (1933-1935)
『映画藝術研究』

Edited by Sasaki Norio, this was a serious criticial journal that particularly focused on aesthetic questions; some articles even topped forty pages in length. A total of eighteen issues were published, many including translations of foreign theoreticians like Eisenstein and Arnheim.

Kikan eiga Ryumiēru = Lumière (1985-1988)
『季刊映画リュミエール = Lumière』

An influential 1980s journal centered around the critic Hasumi Shigehiko. Focused primarily on foreign film, it did devote some issues to Japanese cinema. Starting in the fall of 1985, it ran for fourteen issues until the winter of 1988.

Senzen eizō riron zasshi shūsei
Tokyo: Yumani Shobō, 1989.
『戦前映像理論雑誌集成』ゆまに書房, 1989.
[1-3] *Engeki, eiga* (1926). -- [4-7] *Gekijōgai* (1929-1930). -- [8] *Eiga chishiki* (1929). -- [9-11] *Eiga shūdan* (1935-1938). -- [12-14] *Eigakai* (1938-1940). -- [15-21] *Eiga to ongaku* (1937-1940).

Reprints of some of the important intellectual film journals from the late 1920s to the late 1930s. *Eiga shūdan*, for instance, was a left-oriented theoretical journal edited by Imamura Taihei and Sugiyama Heiichi.

Shinema 69 (1969-1971)
『シネマ69』

The quarterly *Shinema 69* (later *Shinema 70* and *Shinema 71*) set the tone for film criticism after 1970 by rejecting politically based writings or criticism by non-film specialists and advocating looking at film as film. Editors like Yamane Sadao and Hatano Tetsurō, and contributors such as Hasumi Shigehiko and Ueno Kōshi, would come to dominate subsequent film criticism.

Local Film Periodicals

Eiga shinbun (1984-1999)
『映画新聞』

Literally the size and form of a small newspaper and published monthly out of Osaka by editors Kageyama Satoshi and Erikawa Ken, *Eiga shinbun* was a valuable site for expressing alternative opinions on often alternative cinema, and one of the last bastions of the important Japanese intellectual tradition, the *ronsō* (debate), in film journalism.

FB (1993-2004)
『FB』

FB was a coterie magazine that involved many of the film intellectuals of the Kansai region. First appearing in autumn 1993 with issues published two or three times a year, it eventually became an annual publication which was last printed in autumn 2004.

Documentary and Experimental

Bunka eiga kenkyū (1938-1940)
『文化映画研究』

This was one of the fora where the meaning and purpose of the so-called *bunka eiga* was debated.

Kiroku eiga (1958-1964)
『記録映画』

This started out as the official organ of the Kyōiku Eiga Sakka Kyōkai, and the magazine quickly brought debates brewing in their earlier newsletter into very public view. Political struggles over the fate of documentary played out in its pages, resulting first in the name change to Kiroku Eiga Sakka Kyōkai and then to a mass evacuation and creation of a competing organization and journal. *Kiroku eiga* was the forum for many important polemics by directors like Matsumoto Toshio (one of the editors), Ōshima Nagisa, Yoshida Kijū, Noda Shin'kichi, and many influential intellectuals of the day.

Gekkan imēji foramu (1980-1995)
『月刊イメージフォーラム』

A monthly journal published by Dagereo Shuppan, the publishing arm of Image Forum (12), the primary organization in Japan promoting experimental cinema. The journal, then, is largely devoted to experimental work in film and video, but also has quite a number of pieces discussing regular commercial cinema.

General Histories

Previous film historians were among the first to use resources like the ones introduced here to reflect on cinema and attempt to answer questions about the origins, development, and function of the medium in Japan. Their work can serve as a foundation for subsequent historians, establishing various facts and positions that can be carried on. Tanaka Jun'ichirō's histories, for instance, can function as filmographies, an invaluable help when studying especially minor genres like educational film that suffer from poor record keeping. They also constitute collections of primary sources, since Tanaka knew and interviewed many of the primary figures in film's development in Japan. Tsukada Yoshinobu's or Yamamoto Kikuo's research collects secondary sources—mainly newspaper and magazine articles—to painstakingly and empirically answer basic questions (about when and how cinema arrived in Japan, and then how it was seen to be influenced by foreign film). They are thus both anthologies and indexes.

Scholars today can build on their research, question it, or use the sources they cite or reproduce for other purposes. These works, however, as is the case with most histories, were influenced by their historical context and shaped by ideological concerns. Most of the histories produced from the 1920s until the 1980s, for instance, accepted the basic views of the Pure Film Movement, which attempted to modernize cinema in the 1910s from the standpoint of state power and the intellectual classes and assumed that films before that Movement were not cinematic. Such film histories can still be useful, but they may be read less for the facts they provide, than for what they don't provide—less for the interpretations they offer than for the historical conditions influencing such interpretations.

The following selection is restricted to books that may be considered general histories. Most cover at least fifty years of history in considerable detail, and are starting points for other rich studies like those of David Bordwell and David Desser that narrow their focus to smaller topics or chunks of time. This isn't anywhere near comprehensive; rather, they are general histories we use and admire. While there are some good long histories of particular genres like the jidaigeki, *we only introduce here some works on larger categories such the modes of documentary and animation.*

The Best of the Best

The Japanese Film: Art and Industry, by Joseph L. Anderson and

Donald Richie
Princeton: Princeton University Press, 1982.

Considering it was originally written on butcher paper rolls in 1959 and is marred by distasteful Cold War political stances, it is impressive that this exhaustively researched tome has yet to be displaced by a newer book. It is no exaggeration that this sturdiness is extremely rare in film studies. One reason is its close attention to the industrial underpinnings of the art, an angle few authors took back then (or even today). The 1982 expanded edition brought the book up to date, appending some historiographic essays reflecting on the earlier writing. An important essay by Anderson refutes the first edition's disparagement of the *benshi* with some fine-grained research. The book also has a nice bibliography and a curious "family tree" for directors and studios, a long fold-out in the boxed first edition.

Nihon eigashi, zōhoban, by Satō Tadao
Tokyo: Iwanami Shoten, 2006-2007.
佐藤忠男著『日本映画史』増補版，岩波書店，2006-2007.

Satō Tadao is one of the most prolific and powerful critics of the postwar era. He started out his career writing for the journal *Kagaku no shisō*. This periodical's orientation—combining intellectually rigorous essays for everyday readers with a focus on the social significance of popular culture—informed Satō's approach to film criticism, making him one of the most beloved and interesting critics in Japanese film. *Nihon eigashi* was Satō's self-conscious attempt to follow-up, and perhaps displace, Tanaka Jun'ichirō's *Nihon eiga hattatsushi* (see below). This was no matter of competition; Tanaka supported Satō's long project by donating the best materials from his own personal collection (see the entry on Ōta City Nitta Library, pp. 52-53). Indeed, the works are completely different. Tanaka's book is data-heavy, thick with extended quotes, and oriented toward industrial "progress." By way of contrast, Satō's *Nihon eigashi* is the work of an essayist. It is emminently readable and well-researched (although poorly referenced). This is a revised version of the initial 1995 book; its most important addition is the extra decade of film history. The fourth volume contains additional perspectives—particularly essays focusing on themes that span the chronological history of Japanese cinema—as well as a long chronology and an index.

Nihon eiga hattatsushi, by Tanaka Jun'ichirō
Tokyo: Chūō Kōronsha, 1980.
田中純一郎著『日本映画発達史』中央公論社，1980.

This five-volume work is the most important multi-volume film history for

Japanese film studies, even though it tends to offer a kind of history based on the assumptions of the Pure Film Movement. It is the culmination of Tanaka's research on film history begun back in the 1920s, and accomplished through the personal contacts he established from that time through his work as a film journalist and editor. Initially published in serialized article form before the war, the first edition came out in a 3-volume set in 1957. This was followed by a 5-volume set in 1975-1976 (itself reprinted in 1980). It is strong on industry history, but also functions as a filmography and directory of film and industry personnel, as Tanaka often lists important films and important shake ups at the studios. He pays attention to the place of foreign film in Japan, as well as to marginal genres like documentary and the development of film journalism. The last volume includes a chronology that is indexed with his history.

Best Feature Film-Centric

Eiga gojūnenshi, by Hazumi Tsuneo
Tokyo: Masu Shobō, 1942.
筧見恒夫著『映画五十年史』鱒書房, 1942.
Eiga gojūnenshi, by Hazumi Tsuneo
Osaka: Sōgensha, 1951.
筈見恒夫著『映画五十年史』創元社, 1951.

These are fifty-year histories of cinema published ten years apart, and that decade makes quite a difference. The two editions of Hazumi's *Eiga gojūnenshi* are interesting not only in terms of the history they tell, but also in how they are examples of how historiography could change between the wartime and the postwar.

A Hundred Years of Japanese Film, rev. ed., by Donald Richie
Tokyo: Kōdansha, 2005.

Richie's fourth attempt at a general history is his most complex and satisfying. Having moved away from the earlier searches for the genius of auteurs or the expression of national essence, he narrates 100 years of Japanese film history from a variety of angles. The interplay between "representational" and "presentational" styles is a running theme, although it does not overwhelm the book (and thus remains frustratingly undeveloped). Paired with his first effort with Anderson, these two books provide the best English-language starting points for approaching Japanese cinema.

Japanese Cinema: Film Style and National Character, by Donald Richie

New York: Anchor Books, 1971; online version, Ann Arbor: University of Michigan Center for Japanese Studies Publications Program, 2004: www.umich.edu/~iinet/cjs/publications/cjsfaculty/filmrichie.html

This was originally published as a slim book by the Japan Travel Bureau in 1961. The book maps out Japanese cinema against a spectrum from the traditional to the transgressive vis-à-vis "national character." In the electronic reprint, the author properly rejects his categories of "tradition" and "national character"; however, Richie's beautifully-written analyses of films remain worth revisiting.

A New History of Japanese Cinema, by Isolde Standish
New York: Continuum, 2005.

A thematic approach to the general history, this book focuses on issues of modernism, nationalism, imperialism, transgression and gender, the latter progressing from her book *Myth and Masculinity in the Japanese Cinema*. As such it offers a useful outline from a sociological perspective of the central questions brought up by these issues, but many others have worked on these issues as well. The format may be profitably seen as an updating of Joan Mellon's *The Waves at Genji's Door*.

Nihon eiga gendaishi, 2 vols., by Fujita Motohiko
Tokyo: Kashinsha, 1977-1979.
冨士田元彦著『日本映画現代史』花神社, 1977-1979.

These two tomes technically deal with the period between 1935 and 1955, but coupled with Fujita's *Gendai eiga no kiten* (Tokyo: Kinokuniya Shoten, 1965) and *Nihon eigashi no sōshutsu* (Tokyo: Goryū Shoin, 1983), they represent the core of Fujita's concerted effort to outline the historical foundations of Japanese cinema. Also a poet, Fujita participated in the *KineJun Nihon eigashi* (135) and was close to the Waseda method.

Nihon eiga gijutsushi
Tokyo: Nihon Eiga Terebi Gijutsu Kyōkai, 1997.
『日本映画技術史』日本映画テレビ技術協会, 1997.

There has been a lively sector of film publishing centered on the technology of the medium, starting especially with Gonda Yasunosuke (*Katsudō shashin no genri oyobi ōyō* [Tokyo: Uchida Rōkakuho, 1914]) and Kaeriyama Norimasa (eg.

Katsudō shashingeki no sōsaku to satsueihō (Tokyo: Hikōsha, 1917). In the postwar much of this activity circulated around the magazine *Eiga terebi gijutsu*, published by the Motion Picture and Television Engineering Society of Japan. This book is their rendering of Japanese film history from a technological point of view, published to commemorate the film centenary. It has a bibliography, timeline, various narrative histories, and wonderful photographs. There are enough errors in the text that users should cite with care.

Nihon eiga 101-nen: Mirai e no chōsen, by Yamada Kazuo
Tokyo: Shin Nihon Shuppansha,1997.
山田和夫著『日本映画101年　未来への挑戦』新日本出版社, 1980.

Yamada Kazuo is the most prominent old-left film critic of the postwar era, and this is his contribution to the cinema centenary. This isn't the best monograph on Japanese film history, but it's worth noting (and reading) because it's a narration of Japanese film history firmly rooted in a communist perspective, with attention to both industrial structures and grass-roots film and screening movements.

Nihon eiga jūdan, by Takenaka Tsutomu
Tokyo: Shirakawa Shoin, 1974-1976.
竹中労著『日本映画縦断』白川書院, 1974-1976.

The controversal, hard-hitting left-wing journalist Takenaka Tsutomu (a.k.a. Takenaka Rō) turned to film—prewar cinema at that—in this series of three books collecting articles he penned for *Kinema junpō*. It is a series that was never finished. Taking on lesser known film people, including some in interviews, Takenaka offers a version of Japanese film history only he could provide.

Nihon eiga ni okeru gaikoku eiga no eikyō: Hikaku eigashi kenkyū, by Yamamoto Kikuo
Tokyo: Waseda Daigaku Shuppanbu, 1983.
山本喜久男著『日本映画における外国映画の影響　比較映画史研究』早稲田大学出版部, 1983.

This is less Yamamoto's interpretive account of the influence of foreign cinema on Japanese film, based on his own textual analysis, than a precisely researched history of prewar discourse that cited such possible influences. It is a marvellous resource for the history not only of such influences (although Yamamoto only deals with the prewar), but also of the discourse on film in Japan. This can therefore help you find out cases of perceived influence of Soviet cinema, for instance, or when Soviet theory started entering writings on cinema.

Nihon eiga no 80-nen, by Yamada Kazuo
Tokyo: Isseisha, 1976.
山田和夫著『日本映画の80年』一声社, 1976.

This history strongly reflects Yamada's position as a film critic connected to the Japanese Communist Party who focuses on left-wing film movements and social realist cinema but criticizes the New Wave.

Nihon eiga no rekishi: Sono kigyō, gijutsu, geijutsu, by Okada Susumu
Tokyo: Daviddosha, 1967.
岡田晋著『日本映画の歴史 その企業・技術・芸術』ダヴィッド社, 1967.

A rather polemical work that is full of anecdotes, Okada's account is one of the most stylistically dramatic of the histories. An example of the narrativization of film history.

Nihon eigakai jibutsu kigen, by Yoshiyama Kyokkō
Tokyo: "Shinema to Engei" Sha, 1933.
吉山旭光著『日本映畫界事物起源』「シネマと演藝」社, 1933.
Nihon eigashi nenpyō, by Yoshiyama Kyokkō
Tokyo: Eiga Hōkokusha, 1940.
吉山旭光著『日本映畫史年表』映畫報國社, 1940.

Yoshiyama was one of the first film critics, having started writing regularly on movies in the late Meiji. These two works are basically anecdotal histories, full of errors and embellished stories, but yet frequently an intriguing window onto the early film world (or a particular memory of it). Both were reprinted in volume 29 of the *Nihon eigaron gensetsu taikei* (78).

Nihon eigashi, by Iijima Tadashi
Tokyo: Hakusuisha, 1955.
飯島正著『日本映画史』白水社, 1955.

A unique Japanese film history given that the author, a long-active film critic who later taught at Waseda University, tended to focus on foreign cinema and avant-garde film for much of his career. He divides his history into six periods, the first—before the Pure Film Movement—being "Before Film Art." While he covers basic industrial and social trends, his focus is on the films and filmmakers, which he writes about using an impressionist form of criticism that came to dominate much of the history of Japanese film criticism.

Nihon eigashi 100-nen, by Yomota Inuhiko
Tokyo: Shūeisha, 2000.
四方田犬彦著『日本映画史100年』集英社, 2000.

While it's debatable that he really escapes conventional historiography, Yomota's *shinsho*-sized book is refreshing for its interrogation of the assumptions undergirding national cinema study. He points to despised genres, *zainichi* films, production in the colonies, Okinawa-language films—film forms that don't square easily with received notions about "Japanese film." It is short and sweet, and by far the best of the rash of national film histories published for the cinema centenary.

Nihon eigashi: Jissha kara seichō konmei no jidai made, Sekai no eiga sakka, vol. 31
Tokyo: Kinema Junpōsha, 1976.
『日本映画史　実写から成長混迷の時代まで』世界の映画作家: 31、キネマ旬報社, 1976.

An important and in many ways groundbreaking work since it was the first film history compiled by university trained film scholars such as Iwamoto Kenji and Chiba Nobuo. It thus tends to be more meticulous in its documentation and argumentation than previous histories. This was a collaborative work printed as part of a Kinema Junpōsha series and unfortunately was not as widely distributed as it should have been.

Nihon eigashi no kenkyū: Katsudō shashin torai zengo no jijō, by Tsukada Yoshinobu
Tokyo: Gendai Shokan, 1980.
塚田嘉信著『日本映画史の研究　活動写真渡来前後の事情』現代書館, 1980.

While this is not a history that spans at least fifty years, it earns inclusion here as one of the most impressive examples of historiographic legwork. As an independent researcher, Tsukada focused on the early years of cinema in Japan and in this book, he scoured through practically all the newspapers in the first year after the apparatus was imported to determine what was imported, when, by whom, and what happened to each machine afterwards. Since Tsukada reprints most of the articles he finds, this is an invaluable guide to early discourse on cinema.

Ō-Bei oyobi Nihon eigashi, by Ishimaki Yoshio
Tokyo: Puratonsha, 1925.
石巻良夫著『欧米及日本の映画史』プラトン社, 1925.

One of the first monographic film histories, penned by a writer known for his journalistic reporting on the industry. Its focus is thus less on the films than on the business.

To the Distant Observer: Form and Meaning in the Japanese Cinema, by Noël Burch
Berkeley, CA: University of California Press, 1979.
Ann Arbor, MI: University of Michigan Center for Japanese Studies Publications Program, 2006 (www.umich.edu/~iinet/cjs/publications/cjsfaculty/filmburch.html).

Burch's book was a formalist polemic aimed at conventional film historiography, which inevitably began the story of film with a split between Lumière (realism) and Melies (formalism). In a remarkably ambitious argument routed through Japanese film, *To the Distant Observer* proposes that the real division in film history is marked by bourgeois Hollywood realism and progressive political modernism. He identifies a tendency in Japanese film toward formalism, which he reads as a resistance to the aesthetic categories of the West. The book was roundly attacked upon publication, particularly as a handy example of orientalism (Edward Said's book was published in 1978). However, it must be recognized as one of the first attempts to write a history of Asian cinema that resists and critiques the progressive historicism of Euro-American film theory. Aside from many challenging close textual analyses, Burch made a lasting contribution by calling our attention to the riches of the 1930s cinema. He called this a golden age, condemning the 1950s cinema as bourgeois, slavish incorporation of Hollywood realism and its ideological underpinnings. This would make our "Best of the Best" list for general histories, were it not for all the errors in fact and transliteration. A free online reprint is available at the University of Michigan Center for Japanese Studies Publication Program website, with a new introduction by Harry Harootunian.

Best Documentary/Avant-garde/Animation (Everything Else)

Dokyumentarī eiga no genten: Sono shisō to hōhō, by Tanikawa Yoshio
Tokyo: Fūtōsha, 1990.
谷川義雄著『ドキュメンタリー映画の原点』風濤社, 1990.

This, along with Satō Tadao's *Nihon dokyumentarī eizōshi* (see below), is the canonical history of Japanese documentary. It updates previous editions printed in 1971 and 1977.

Japanese Documentary Film: The Meiji Era Through Hiroshima, by Abé Mark Nornes
Minneapolis: University of Minnesota Press, 2003.
Forest of Pressure: Ogawa Shinsuke and Postwar Japanese Documentary
Minneapolis: University of Minnesota Press, 2007.

Markus originally conceived these two books as a single-volume history of Japanese documentary, but his mentor wisely asked him to split it up. The first book looks more like a general history, but read together they do constitute a narration of the documentary form—in practice and theory—from the beginning of cinema through the 1990s.

Japanese Experimental Film & Video 1955-1994, edited by Image Forum
Osaka: Kirin Plaza Osaka, 1994.
イメージフォーラム編『日本実験映像40年史』キリンプラザ大阪, 1994.

This is the bilingual (English/Japanese) catalog from a program of experimental films curated by Image Forum, and thus weighted towards filmmakers associated with that institution. It has lists of canonical films with synopses, short filmmaker profiles, a timeline, and nice essays by Kawanaka Nobuhiro, Suzuki Shirōyasu, Nishijima Norio among others.

Nihon animēshon eigashi, by Yamaguchi Katsunori and Watanabe Yasushi
Osaka: Yūbunsha, 1977.
山口且訓, 渡辺泰著『日本アニメーション映画史』有文社, 1977.

Except for the fact that it is now thirty years old, this is the most important history of animation in Japan. Not only do the authors, with the help of the Planet Film Archive (15-16), thoroughly narrate the complex artistic and industrial history of Japanese animation, but they quite rigorously provide a chronologically ordered filmography of all the animated films they could account for at the time, one that includes not only credits but sometimes detailed commentary, stills and plot summaries. The same authors issued a supplement, *Animēshon sakuhin mokuroku 1977-1987*, in 1987 that updates this filmography.

Nihon kiroku eizōshi, by Satō Tadao
Tokyo: Hyōronsha, 1977.
佐藤忠男著『日本記録映像史』評論社, 1977.

Like much of Satō's work, this is a remarkably uneven book. As a general introduction to Japanese nonfiction film it has its place.

Nihon kyōiku eiga hattatsushi, by Tanaka Jun'ichirō
Tokyo: Kagyūsha, 1979.
田中純一郎著『日本教育映画発達史』蝸牛社, 1979.

Given the vagaries in the nomenclature for documentary cinema in Japan, *"kyōiku eiga"* here refers as much to documentary as to strictly educational cinema. Since relatively few records exist of educational and documentary film, this is not just a history but an invaluable filmography of a too-often ignored genre. If you are trying to find out about a minor documentary film, this is the first place to look. The historiographic approach of this history of the "educational film" is very close to Tanaka's *Nihon eiga hattasushi,* meaning lots of quoting and short film synopses. It was essentially written as a companion piece to the other book, although he relied less on interviews and more on published materials. Despite the title, it covers most of the other genres of documentary and is particularly good at outlining the institutional background of the form. Includes an index and a handy timeline (1899-1975).

Nihon no anime zenshi: Sekai o seishita Nihon anime no kiseki, by Yamaguchi Yasuo
Tokyo: Ten Bukkusu, 2004.
山口康男著『日本のアニメ全史　世界を制した日本アニメの奇跡』テン・ブックス, 2004.

This is clearly the work of an insider. Yamaguchi worked at Tōei Dōga in the 1960s, spending 40 years in the business. He worked in virtually every role in the studio and participated in the labor actions of the day, so this history of Japanese animation pays close attention to industrial practice, labor issues, and the impact of new technologies on both aesthetics and workflow patterns. The mix makes for a very interesting history. The back of the book includes a chronology, terminology glossary, and flowcharts describing workflow, industrial organization and series runs.

Nihon no kagaku eigashi, by Tanikawa Yoshio
Tokyo: Yuni Tsūshinsha, 1978.
谷川義雄著『日本の科学映画史』ユニ通信社, 1978.

This supplements Tanaka Jun'ichirō's *Nihon kyōiku eiga hattatsushi* (139) and Tanikawa's *Dokyumentarī eiga no genten: Sono shisō to hōhō* (137) by limiting itself to the science film. The choice makes sense, as this is a highly coherent genre of the documentary in Japan and until recently it enjoyed far more prestige than in other national contexts.

Guides to Archives

Eiga mokuroku 1999-nen
Tokyo: Tokyo-toritsu Hibiya Toshokan, 2000.
『映画目録』東京都立日比谷図書館, 2000.

This is a widely-held index to Hibiya Public Library's 16mm film collection (39-40). They now have an online database. However, the online catalog is not complete so it may worth paging through this if one is searching hard for documentaries. With nearly 10,000 films, Hibiya is a significant collection and it is also extremely easy to use.

Films in the Collection of the Pacific Film Archive, Volume I: Daiei Motion Picture Co., Ltd. Japan
Berkeley: University Art Museum, 1979.

This an essential guide to the Daiei holdings at the Pacific Film Archives, a strong collection with English subtitles (25-26). Unfortunately, this was the fruit of a small grant and they never managed to publish Volume II. The entries list credits, release titles, and lengthy synopses. The latter are credited and written especially for this book. Notably, the entries end with bibliographic references, short critiques, keywords, and evaluations of the subtitles and print condition. Of course, the latter bit of information is no longer reliable; word on the street is that the PFA's Daiei and Nikkatsu collection is beginning to suffer the inevitability of print rot—changing colors and the sick fragrance of vinegar. Until the cans contain nothing but dust, this remains one of the truly precious archival resources we have.

Firumu Sentā shozō eiga mokuroku: Nihon gekieiga
Tokyo: Tokyo Kokuritsu Kindai Bijutsukan, 2001.
『フィルムセンター所蔵映画目録　日本劇映画』東京国立近代美術館, 2001.

This thick catalog of the National Film Center's films looks impressive, but doesn't come close to adequately listing their holdings. It's a start, we suppose, but this is a far richer archive than one would gather from this book (and its earlier incarnation in 1986). Since their online database covers their collection better, this catalog now functions best as a filmography since each entry provides precise cast, staff and other information.

Nihon ni okeru senzenki no eizō shiryō no shozai kakutei to taitoru no dētabēsu, by Yamada Akira
Tokyo: Meiji Daigaku, 1997.

山田朗著『日本における戦前期の映像史料の所在確定とタイトルのデータベース化』明治大学, 1997.

This is an index of the newsreels of the prewar era preserved in the National Film Center (23-25), produced as a report on research funded by the Ministry of Education's Kagaku Kenkyūhi Hojokin.

"Okinawa-ken Kōbunshokan ni okeru Okinawa kankei eizō shiryō," by Nakachi Hiroshi
Okinawa-ken Kōbunshokan kenkyū kiyō 2 (March 2000): 153-180.
中地弘志著「沖縄県公文書館に於ける沖縄関係映像資料」『沖縄県公文書館研究紀要』2号(3月2000年): 153-180.

An invaluable map of all the archives in Japan and the visual materials they have collected regarding Okinawa.

Shozō eiga tōroku
Kawasaki City: Kawasaki-shi Shimin Myūjiamu, 1989.
『所蔵映画登録』川崎市市民ミュージアム, 1989.
Eiga, bideo sakuhin shūshū mokuroku
Kawasaki City: Kawasaki-shi Shimin Myūjiamu Eizō Bumon, 1989.
『映画、ビデオ作品収集目録』川崎市市民ミュージアム映像部門, 1989.

Kawasaki City Museum published these two indexes the same year. The first is on glossy paper and features pretty pictures of 168 films, most of them features. The second index looks spare, but includes well over a thousand titles from documentary, animation, television and video art. Happily, these are hopelessly out of date as their collection expanded and they became one of the larger film archives in Japan.

"Zaibeikoku Okinawa kankei shiryō chōsa shūshū katsudō hōkoku II: Beikoku Kokuritsu Kōbunshokan Shinkan shozō no eizō, onsei shiryō hen," by Nakamoto Kazuhiko
Okinawa-ken Kōbunshokan kenkyū kiyō 9 (March 2007): 17-26.
仲本和彦著「在米国沖縄関係資料調査収集活動報告II:米国国立公文書館新館所蔵の映像、音声資料編」『沖縄県公文書館研究紀要』9号(3月2007年): 17-26.

This article explains what materials were acquired from the U.S. National Archives (14-15). With its detailed information on the record groups from the Occupation era, users of NARA will also find it extremely valuable.

Local Histories

Among the underused resources in Japanese film studies, one of the most unusual is a lively genre of local histories. Too often "Japanese film" is thought of in the singular. This is undoubtedly a product of the national bias in foreign film study. Heterogeneous film cultures are homogenized around certain centers, in this case Kyoto and Tokyo. And while it is true that the vast majority of films have been produced by companies located in those cities, there have been local productions as well, especially in independent film. More importantly, there have been distinct, vibrant film cultures in localities throughout Japan centered especially on exhibition, something that is attested to by the large number of books produced about these places. Some are just celebrations of the works that happened to have been filmed in those locations, but many concentrate on local theater districts, distribution arms, film circles, regulations, bigwigs, etc. There are even books devoted to single theaters. All these books can serve as a valuable guide to the movie-going experience outside Tokyo. Many are chocked full of pictures and some include reprints of local theater programs and chirashi. *Ever since the emergence of reception studies in the 1980s, we have been waiting for some intrepid researcher to make use of these wonderful histories. Here is a strong sample, arranged by prefecture.*

Aichi: Sawai Kiyoshi, *Mini-goraku eigashi: Nagoya Ōsu kaiwai no omoide* (Tokyo: Shinpūsha, 2007); Itō Shiei, *Shinema yoru hiru: kaikō Nagoya eigashi: 80m/m kara 70m/m made* (Nagoya: Itō Shiei, 1984); Watanabe Tsunao, *Nagoya no eiga: Shihan* (Nagoya: Sakkasha, 1961).

Aomori: *Aomori shinema paradaisu* (Aomori: Tōō Nippōsha, 1996).

Ehime: *Ehime eiga rokēshon nabi* (Matsuyama: Ehime-ken Kankōka, 2004).

Fukui: Sugimoto Isami, *Fukui eigashi* (Fukui: Fukui Eiga Sākuru Kyōgikai, 1972).

Fukuoka: *Back to the Movies: Fukuoka-shi no eiga to eigakan, 100-nen no ayumi* (Fukuoka: Ashi Shobō, 1995); Nōma Yoshihiro, *Fukuoka Hakata eiga hyakunen: Eiga to eigakan no kōbō shiwa* (Tsukuba: Imamura Shoten Sankureito, 2003); *Kyūshū shinema paradaisu* (Fukuoka: Fukuhaku Sōgō Insatsu, 2000); Nōma Yoshihiro, *Zusetsu Fukuoka-ken eigashi hakkutsu: Senzen hen* (Tokyo: Kokusho Kankōkai, 1984).

Hokkaidō: Takeoka Wadao, *Eiga no naka no Hokkaidō* (Sapporo: Hokkaidō Shinbunsha, 1991); Sarashina Genzō, *Hokkaidō eigashi* (Sapporo: Kushima, 1970); Sarashina Genzō, *Hokkaidō katsudō shashin shōshi* (Sapporo: Kushima Kōgyō, 1960); *Sapporo to eiga* (Sapporo: Hokkaidō Shinbunsha, 1989; Kuroda Shin'ichi, *Yume no binetsu: Sapporo Jabb 70 Hall no 10-nenkan* (Tokyo: Hon no Zasshisha, 1993).

Hyōgō: Asada Shūichi, *Kōbe saigo no eigakan* (Akashi: Gendō Shuppan, 2001); *Kōbe to shinema no isseiki* (Kōbe: Kōbe Shinbun Sōgō Shuppan Sentā, 1998).

Ishikawa: Ishikawa Eiga Bunka Kyōkai, ed., *Kanazawa shinema 30-nen*

(Kanazawa: Hokkoku Shuppansha, 1984).

Iwate: Moriuchi Masashi, *Morioka eiga konjaku* (Tonanmura, Iwate: Chihō Kōronsha, 1976).

Kagawa: *Omoide no Kagawa eigashi* (Takamatsu: Kagawa-ken Kōgyō Kankyō Eisei Dōgyō Kumiai, 1992).

Kanagawa: Maruoka Sumio, *Kanagawa shinema fudoki* (Yokohama: Kanagawa Shinbunsha, 1993); Maruoka Sumio, *Odeonza monogatari* (Yokohama: Mutsuzaki Akira, 1975); *Shinema shiti: Yokohama to eiga* (Yokohama: Yokohama Toshi Hatten Kinenkan, 2005).

Kōchi: Yamamoto Yoshihiro, *Kōchi no jishu jōei kara: "Eiga to hanasu" kairo o motomete* (Osaka: Eiga Shinbun, 1996).

Kumamoto: Kumamoto Daigaku Eiga Bunkashi Kōza, ed., *Eiga kono hyakunen: Chihō kara no shiten* (Kumamoto: Kumamoto Shuppan Bunka Kaikan, 1995); *Kumamoto shinema kōdan* (Kumamoto: Seichōsha, 1978); Inoue Tomoshige, *Kyūshū Okinawa shinema fudoki* (Kumamoto: Kumamoto Shuppan Bunka Kaikan, 1995).

Kyoto: Hoshikawa Seiji, *Daiei Kyōto Satsueijo katsudōya hanjōki* (Tokyo: Nihon Keizai Shinbusha, 1997); Nakajima Sadao, et al., *Eiga roman kikō: Kyōto shinemappu* (Kyoto: Kyōto Kokusai Eigasai Soshiki Iinkai Kyōto Jimukyoku, 1994); Shōbayashi Fumio, *Kyōto eiga sangyōron: Inobēshon e no chōsen* (Kyoto: Keibunsha, 1994); Toki Akihiro, Kyōto Kinema Tanteidan, eds., *Kyōto eiga zue: Nihon eiga wa Kyōto kara hajimatta* (Tokyo: Firumu Ātosha, 1994); *Kyōto no eiga 80-nen no ayumi* (Kyoto: Kyōto Shinbunsha, 1980); Ōta Yoneo, Mizuguchi Kaoru, and Toki Akihiro, *Nihon eiga to Kyōto: Kyōto eiga hyakunen kinen* (Tokyo: Heibonsha, 1997); Kurata Toshiaki, *Shinema no Kyōto o tadoru* (Kyoto: Tankōsha, 2007); *Tōei Uzumasa Eigamura: Jidaigeki eiga no furusato zengaido* (Tokyo: Bijutsu Shuppansha, 1997); "Nihon eiga to Kyōto," special issue of *Taiyō* 97 (Spring 1997).

Mie: *Kyoshōtachi no fūkei: Mie shinema jijō Ozu Yasujirō, Kinugasa Teinosuke, Fujita Toshiya* (Ise: Ise Bunkasha, 2002); Mizuno Masamitsu and Nobori Shigeki, *Shinema Sukuea Rekku o mō ichido: Aru eigakan no monogatari* (Tokyo: Shinpūsha, 2002)

Miyagi: Shūdan MISSA, ed., *Sendai eiga daizenshū* (Sendai: Imano Heiban Insatsu, 1982).

Nagasaki: *Nagasaki enkei gekijō: Shōsetsu, eiga, butai no naka no Nagasaki* (Nagasaki: Nagasaki Shinbunsha, 2004).

Niigata: Niigata Shimin Eigakan Kanshōkai, ed., *Machi no kioku, gekijō no akari: Niigata-ken eigakan to kankyaku no rekishi* (Niigata-shi: Niigata Shimin Eigakan Kanshōkai, 2007).

Okayama: Matsuda Sadakazu, *Okayama no eiga* (Okayama: Nihon Bunkyō Shuppan, 1983).

Okinawa: Yamazato Masato, *An'yatasa!: Okinawa, sengo no eiga 1945-1955* (Naha: Niraisha, 2001); Iki Ichirō, *Eizō bunkaron: Okinawa hatsu* (Naha: Tōyō Kikaku, 2000); Inoue Tomoshige, *Kyūshū Okinawa shinema fudoki*

(Kumamoto: Kumamoto Shuppan Bunka Kaikan, 1995); Yomota Inuhiko and Ōmine Sawa, *Okinawa eigaron* (Tokyo: Sakuhinsha, 2008); Nakazato Isao, Hama Haruka, and Itō Shigeaki, eds., *Ryūkyū Reflections: Nexus of Borders* (Yamagata: Yamagata International Documentary Film Festival Organizing Committee, 2003).

Osaka: Takabe Yoshinobu, *Zenbu Ōsaka no eiga yanen* (Tokyo: Heibonsha, 2000); *Eizō ni miru Ōsaka no michi* (Osaka: Ōsaka-shi Doboku Gijutsu Kyōkai, 1997).

Tokushima: Bandō Tetsuo and Itō Tetsuo, *Tokushima eiga sandaiki* (Tokushima: Tokushima-ken Kyōikukai Shuppanbu, 1965).

Tokyo: Satō Tadao, *Eiga no naka no Tōkyō* (Tokyo: Heibonsha, 2002); Kawamoto Saburō, *Ginmaku no Tōkyō: Eiga de yomigaeru Shōwa* (Tokyo: Chūō Kōronsha, 1999); Miura Daishirō, *Jinseiza sanjūgonenshi: Yakeato kara Bungeiza made* (Tokyo: Jinseiza, 1983); Shinjuku-ku Rekishi Hakubutsukan, ed., *Kinema no tanoshimi: Shinjuku Musashinokan no ōgon jidai* (Tokyo: Shinjuku Kyōiku Iinkai, 1992); Tomita Hitoshi, *Tōkyō eiga meisho zukan* (Tokyo: Heibonsha, 1992); Fumikura Heizaburō, *Tōkyō ni okeru katsudō shashin*, Nihon eigaron gensetsu taikei 27 (Tokyo: Yumani Shobō, 2006); Satō Tadao, *Tōkyō to iu shuyaku: Eiga no naka no Edo, Tōkyō* (Tokyo: Kōdansha, 1988).

Yamagata: Tomitsuka Masaki, ed., *Films about Yamagata* (Yamagata: Yamagata International Documentary Film Festival, 2007); Eda Tadashi, *Yonezawa katsudō shashin monogatari*, 2 vols. (Yonezawa: Yonezawa Bunka Konwakai, 1972-1974).

Studio and Production Company Histories

With an industry that has been vertically integrated and supported by block booking for most of its history, Japanese cinema has been particularly centered on the studio or company as a fundamental unit of not only production, but also reception. Major studios have been powerful entities, capable of squeezing out indepenent producers in periods like the 1950s, and developing a variety of non-film businesses like baseball teams and real estate. They also have developed distinct studio film styles and proprietary genres that attract audiences (one could even argue that genres are more tied to studios than they are in the American industry). One thus cannot study major aspects of Japanese film without taking in the particularities of individual companies and the larger industrial structure. As a reflection of this fact, there are a considerable number of books about studios and companies, their business practices and the kinds of films they make. We list those we haven't mentioned elsewhere in the book. These publications are essentially of two kinds: those produced by the companies themselves, and those produced independently by film critics, scholars or industry veterans. Companies did print magazines for their fans during the heyday of the studio era, but like other corporate entities in Japan, they also published limited edition histories on the occasion of an important anniversary. These can sometimes recycle previous editions, be stuffy and understandably biased towards the studio, but they can be chocked full of statistics, filmographies, and corporate details. Some are beautifully designed (like Kuronikuru Tōei*) and some, such as the Shōchiku eighty-year history, produced by major scholars like Tanaka Jun'ichirō. Compiled at different stages in time, their very format and style can tell you a lot about a changing industry. We have also included works produced by labor unions at these studios. Histories produced by outsiders can obviously be more critical, but most are less about the business than about the company as a cultural or cinematic phenomenon, a unit of artistic production or audience reception. They can thus help a variety of film studies, such as auteur analysis, genre study, popular cinema research, and reception studies.*

Many of these are fun to read, filled with wonderful photographs (though we mostly don't list those that are primarily photographs, like the many that Waizu Shuppan has printed), and are often rich with both historical narrative and data on films. One American library with a special collection of company histories is Ohio State University, but the major histories should all be easily available through interlibrary loan.

Daiei

Daiei jūnenshi (Tokyo: Daiei Kabushiki Kaisha, 1951).
Hoshikawa Seiji, *Daiei Kyōto Satsueijo katsudōya hanjōki* (Tokyo: Nihon Keizai Shinbunsha, 1997).
Hayashi Tsuchitarō, *Eiga rokuon gishi hitosuji ni ikite: Daiei Kyōto rokujūnen* (Tokyo: Sōshisha, 2007).

Nikkatsu

Yamane Sadao, ed., *Kannō no puroguramu pikuchua: Roman poruno, 1971-1982 zen eiga* (Tokyo: Firumu Ātosha, 1983).
Nikkatsu Rōdō Kumiai Kessei Jūninenshi Henshū Iinkai, ed., *Kessei jūninen* (Tokyo: Nikkatsu Rōdo Kumiai, 1960).
Ōshita Eiji, *Minna Nikkatsu Akushon ga suki datta* (Tokyo: Kōsaidō Shuppan, 1999).
Nikkatsu (Tokyo: Gendai Kigyō Kenkyūkai, 1962).
Watanabe Takenobu, *Nikkatsu Akushon no kareina sekai*, 3 vols. (Tokyo: Miraisha, 1981-1982).
Nozawa Kazuma, *Nikkatsu 1954-1971: Eizō o sōzōsuru samuraitachi* (Tokyo: Waizu Shuppan, 2000).
Itamochi Takashi, *Nikkatsu eiga kōbō no 80-nen* (Tokyo: Nihon Eiga Terebi Purodyūsā Kyōkai, 1999).
Ishiwari Osamu, *Nikkatsu jidaigeki* (Tokyo: Waizu Shuppan, 2002).
Kamo Reidō, *Nikkatsu no shashi to gensei* (Tokyo: Nikkatsu no Shashi to Gensei Kankōkai, 1930).
Nikkatsu Tamagawa shi (Tokyo: Nikkatsu Tamagawa Satsueijo, 1942).

Nikkatsu shijūnenshi (Tokyo: Nikkatsu Kabushiki Kaisha, 1952).

Nikkatsu gojūnenshi (Tokyo: Nikkatsu Kabushiki Kaisha, 1962).

Matsushima Toshiyuki, *Nikkatsu roman poruno zenshi: Meisaku, meiyū, meikantokutachi* (Tokyo: Kōdansha, 2000).

Roman Poruno o Aisuru Kai, ed., *Nikkatsu Roman teikoku no gyakushū* (Tokyo: Seisei Shuppan, 1997).

Mark Schilling, *No Borders, No Limits: Nikkatsu Action Cinema* (Godalming, England: FAB, 2007).

Shōchiku

Masumoto Kinen, *Jinbutsu Shōchiku eigashi: Kamata no jidai* (Tokyo: Heibonsha, 1987).

Tsukimura Yoshiharu, *Kamata Satsueijo to sono fukin* (Tokyo: Tokyo Mahiro Insatsu, 1972).

Kinema no seiki: Eiga no hyakunen, Shōchiku no hyakunen (Tokyo: Shōchiku Eizō Honbu Eizō Shōgaishitsu, 1995.

Fujitani Yōetsu, *Maboroshi no den'en toshi kara Shōchiku eiga toshi e: Taishō, Shōwa no Ōfuna-chō no kioku kara: Kyōdō shiryō tenjikai hōkokusho* (Kamakura: Kamakura-shi Chūō Toshokan Kindaishi Shiryō Shūshū-shitsu, 2005).

Mitsuyo Wada-Marciano, *Nippon Modern: Japanese Cinema of the 1920s and 1930s* (Honolulu: University of Hawai'i Press, 2009).

Morita Kyōhei and Ōmine Toshinobu, *Omoide 55-wa Shōchiku Ōfuna satsueijo* (Tokyo: Shūeisha, 2004).

Masumoto Kinen, *Shōchiku eiga no eikō to hōkai: Ōfuna no jidai* (Tokyo: Heibonsha, 1988).

Shōchiku hachijūnenshi (Tokyo: Shōchiku Kabushiki Kaisha, 1975).

Shōchiku hyakujūnenshi (Tokyo: Shōchiku Kabushiki Kaisha, 2006).

Shōchiku hyakunenshi (Tokyo: Shōchiku Kabushiki Kaisha, 1996).

Shōchiku kyūjūnenshi (Tokyo: Shōchiku Kabushiki Kaisha, 1985).

Shōchiku nanajūnenshi (Tokyo: Shōchiku Kabushiki Kaisha, 1964).

Yokomizo Tatsuhiko, *Shōchiku no uchimaku* (Tokyo: Kengensha, 1957).

Yoshimura Hideo, *Shōchiku Ōfuna eiga* (Saitama-ken Tokorozawa-shi: Sōdosha, 2000).

Yamanouchi Shizuo, *Shōchiku Ōfuna Satsueijo oboegaki* (Kamakura-shi: Kamakura Shunjūsha, 2003).

Tōei

Tōei Tōkyō Seisakujo Tōsō Kiroku Iinkai, ed., *Eiga no rōdōshatachi: shashin to shōgen: Tōei Tōkyō Satsueijo, 1964.6.19-1985.10.1* (Tokyo: Tōei Rōdō Kumiai, 1990).

Okada Shigeru, *Kuinaki waga eiga jinsei: Tōei to tomoni ayunda 50-nen* (Tokyo: Zaikai Kenkyūjo, 2001).

Kawasaki Hiroshi, *Kuruoshii yume furyōsei kando no Nihon eiga: Tōei sankaku māku ni naze horeta* (Osaka: Seishinsha, 2003).
Takahashi Satoshi, *Muhō chitai: Tōei jitsuroku yakuza eiga* (Tokyo: Ōta Shuppan, 2003).
Tōei Animēshon 50-nenshi: 1956-2006 (Tokyo: Tōei Animēshon, 2006).
Tōei Dōga, ed., *Tōei Dōga chōhen anime daizenshū*, 2 vols. (Tokyo: Tokuma Shoten, 1978).
Tōei gonen no ayumi (Tokyo: Tōei Kabushiki Kaisha, 1956).
Tōei jūnenshi: 1951-nen - 1961-nen (Tokyo: Tōei Kabushiki Kaisha, 1962).
Tōei eiga sanjūnen: Ano hi, ano toki, ano eiga (Tokyo: Tōei Kabushiki Kaisha, 1981).
Kuronikuru Tōei 1947-1991 (Tokyo: Tōei Kabushiki Kaisha, 1992).
Tōei Uzumasa Eigamura Eiga Shiryōkan, ed., *Tōei Kyōto terebi eiga 25-nen* (Kyoto: Tōei Kyōto Sutajio, 1982).

Tōhō

Inoue Masao, *Bunka to tōsō: Tōhō sōgi 1946-1948* (Tokyo: Shinyōsha, 2007).
Gojira gahō: Tōhō gensō eiga hanseiki no ayumi (Tokyo: Take Shobō, 1999).
Onchi Hideo, *'Kinuta' satsueijo to boku no seishun* (Tokyo: Bungei Shunjū, 1999).
Itō Masakazu, *Kiri to toride: Tōhō daisōgi no kiroku* (Tokyo: Rengō Tsūshinsha, 1965).
Tōhō eiga jūnenshishō (Tokyo: Tōhō Eiga, 1942).
Tōhō sanjūnenshi (Tokyo: Tōhō Kabushiki Kaisha, 1963).
Tōhō gojūnenshi (Tokyo: Tōhō Kabushiki Kaisha, 1982).
Tōhō 70-nen eiga, engeki, terebi, bideo sakuhin risuto: 2002-nendo han (Tokyo: Tōhō, 2002).
Takase Masahiro, *Tōhō kantoku gunzō: Kinuta no seishun* (Tokyo: Tōhō, 2005).
Takase Masahiro, *Tōhō Kinuta Satsueijo* (Tokyo: Tōhō, 2004).
Saitō Tadao, *Tōhō kōshinkyoku: Watakushi no satsueijo sendenbu 50-nen* (Tokyo: Heibonsha, 1987).
Stuart Galbraith IV, *The Toho Studios Story: A History and a Complete Filmography* (Lanham, M.D.: Scarecrow Press, 2008).
Tōhō tokusatsu eiga zenshi (Tokyo: Tōhō Shuppan Jigyōshitsu, 1983).

Tōwa

Tōwa Shōji Gōshi Kaisha shashi: Shōwa sannen - Shōwa jūshichinen (Tokyo: Tōwa Shōji Gōshi Kaisha, 1942).
Tōwa Eiga no ayumi 1928-1955 (Tokyo: Tōwa Eiga Kabushiki Kaisha, 1955).
Tōwa no 40-nen: 1928-1968 (Tokyo: Tōwa, 1968).
Tōwa no hanseiki, 1928-1978 (Tokyo: Tōhō Tōwa, 1978).
Tōwa no 60-nen shō (Tokyo: Tōhō Tōwa, 1988).

Smaller Production Companies

Roland Domenig, ed., *Art Theatre Guild: Unabhängiges Japanisches Kino 1962-1984* (Vienna: Vienna International Film Festival, 2003).

Ushida Ayami, *ATG eiga + Shinjuku: Toshi kūkan no naka no eigatachi!* (Tokyo: D Bungaku Kenkyūkai, 2007).

Ogasawara Masakatsu and Satō Masataka, eds., *ATG eiga no zenbō: Gaikoku eiga hen* (Tokyo: Natsu Shokan, 1980).

Satō Tadao, ed., *ATG eiga o yomu: 60-nendai ni hajimatta meisaku no ākaibu* (Tokyo: Firumu Ātosha, 1991).

Taga Shōsuke, *ATG henshū kōki: Kaisō no eigajintachi* (Tokyo: Heibonsha, 1995).

Roland Domenig, ed., *ATG Symposium: Against the Grain: Changes in Japanese Cinema of the 1960s and Early 1970s* (Vienna: Akademischer Arbeitskreis Japan, 2005).

Ogasawara Masakatsu and Satō Masataka, *Āto Shiatā: ATG eiga no zenbō: Nihon eiga* (Tokyo: Natsu Shokan, 1986).

Kuzui Kinshirō, *Āto Shiatā Shinjuku Bunka: Kieta gekijō* (Tokyo: Sōryūsha, 1986).

Tōei Uzumasa Eigamura Eiga Shiryōkan, ed., *Chiezō eiga* (Kyoto: Tōei Kyōto Sutajio, 1980).

Tomita Mika, ed., *Chie Puro jidai* (Tokyo: Firumu Ātosha, 1997).

Tsuji Hisakazu, *Chūka Den'ei shiwa: Ippeisotsu no Nitchū eiga kaisōki, 1939-1945* (Tokyo: Gaifūsha, 1987).

Daito Eiga Kabushiki Kaisha enkakushi (Tokyo: Daito Eiga, 1939).

Natsukashi no Daito eiga: Mō hitotsu no eigashi: shashinshū (Tokyo: Nōberu Shobō, 1992).

Dentsū Eigasha Shashi Shuppan Iinkai, ed., *Sanjūnen no ayumi* (Tokyo: Dentsū Eigasha, 1973)

Kusakabe Kyūshirō, *Eizō o tsukuru hito to kigyō: Iwanami Eiga no sanjūnen* (Tokyo: Mizuumi Shobō, 1980).

Okamoto Masao, *Bunka eiga jidai: Jūjiya Eigabu no hitobito* (Tokyo: Yuni Tsūshinsha, 1996).

Kindai Eiga Kyōkai no 30-nen, 1950-1980 (Tokyo: Kindai Eiga Kyōkai, 1980).

Akai Sukeo and Maruo Toshirō, eds., *Chanbara ōkoku Kyokutō* (Tokyo: Waizu Shuppan, 1998).

Yamaguchi Takeshi, *Aishū no Manshū eiga: Manshūkoku ni saita katsudōyatachi no sekai* (Tokyo: Santen Shobō, 2000).

Yamaguchi Takeshi, *Maboroshi no kinema Man'ei: Amakasu Masahiko to katsudōya gunzō* (Tokyo: Heibonsha, 1989).

Hu Chang and Gu Quan, *Man'ei: Kokusaku eiga no shosō* (Tokyo: Pandora, 1999).

Manshū no kiroku: Man'ei firumu ni utsusareta Manshū (Tokyo: Shūeisha, 1995).

Koizumi Gorō, *Waga seishun to Man'ei* (Tokyo: Gentōsha, 1982).

Misono Kyōhei, ed., *Kaisô Makino Eiga* (Tokyo: Makino Shōzō Sensei Ken'eikai, 1971).

Makino Eiga no jidai: Toyota-shi Kyōdo Shiryōkan shozō eiga shiryō mokuroku (Toyota: Toyota-shi Kyōiku Iinkai, 1996).

Ishiwari Osamu, *Makino ikka* (Tokyo: Waizu Shuppan, 2000).

Segawa Yoshi, *Makino Purodakushon kotohajime* (Kyoto: Shirakawa Shoin, 1977).

Mizuno Shinkō, *Ōsaka Mainichi Shinbun katsudō shashinshi* (Osaka: Ōsaka Mainichi Shinbunsha, 1925).

Riken Kagaku Eiga sōritsu goshūnen (Tokyo: Riken Kagaku Eiga, 1943).

Murayama Eiji, et al., *Sakura Eiga no shigoto: 1955-1991* (Tokyo: Sakura Eigasha, 1992).

Satō Tadao, Togawa Naoki and Maruo Sadamu, *Shinkō Kinema: Senzen goraku eiga no ōkoku* (Tokyo: Yamaji Fumiko Bunka Zaidan, 1993).

Nachi Shirō and Shigeta Toshiyuki, eds., *Ayakashi Ōkura Shin Tōhō* (Tokyo: Waizu Shuppan, 2001).

Natsukashi no Shin Tōhō: Shashin de miru eigashi (Tokyo: Nōberu Shobō, 1994).

Suzuki Yoshiaki, *Shin Tōhō hiwa Izumida Hiroshi no sekai* (Osaka: Puraza, 2001).

Kazami Hayato and Tōkyō Anime Kenkyūkai, *Sutajio Jiburi no himitsu*, 2nd ed. (Tokyo: Dēta Hausu, 2008)

Sutajio Jiburi sakuhin kanren shiryōshū = Archives of Studio Ghibli, 5 vols. (Tokyo: Tokuma Shoten, 1996-1997).

Takarazuka Eiga Seisakujo: Yomigaeru eiga no machi Takarazuka (Kōbe: Kōbe Shinbun Sōgō Shuppan Sentā, 2001).

Sasaki Kan'ichirô, *Teikine den: Jitsuroku Nihon eigashi* (Tokyo: Kindai Bungeisha, 1996).

Uda Tadashi, *Shōwa shoki no Teikoku Kinema* (Higashiōsaka: Higashiōsaka-shi, 1998)

Tōkyō Mūbī, ed., *Tōkyō Mūbī anime taizenshi = Tokyo Movie Anime Super Data File* (Tokyo: Tatsumi Shuppan, 1999).

Yokohama Shinema Shōkai no gyōseki: Eiga sakuhin mokuroku, 1923-1945 (Yokohama: Yokohama-shi Kanagawa Toshokan, 1998).

V. Online and Digital Resources

General Databases

One of the premises of this bibliography is that online resources are far from sufficient to conduct serious research on Japanese film, and thus that it is still necessary for scholars to learn how to manage the complicated maze of published resources and do the legwork necessary to consult paper research tools. That does not mean that internet resources are useless. They are easy to consult and can serve as one avenue to useful information. However, given their mistakes, which of course are not exclusive to internet resources, they just have to be used in conjunction with other published resources.

First a caveat: for databases of books and journals, the resources below are currently the top sources. However, as with everything digital, the leaders of the horse race change yearly. Ask your reference librarian for the latest winners. The subscription-only databases are available at most Japanese libraries; unfortunately, only the largest and richest foreign Asia libraries can afford the ongoing expense of these subscriptions or CD-ROMs.

While we won't offer separate entries, we do want to point out that all the major newspapers have either CD-ROM or online databases, many providing the full-text. This makes newspaper criticism, interviews, and mainstream reportage one of the easiest areas to research.

The Best

FIAF
www.fiafnet.org/uk/publications/fdbo.cfm

FIAF is the global organization of film archives. Their online database is the go-to resource for anything from film periodicals. While it has impressive coverage of non-English languages, there are extremely few Japanese journals here (we would be shocked if it weren't so typical). However, for articles on Japanese film in foreign film periodicals, this should be one's first stop. Subscription only; included in Proquest.

Google Book Search
books.google.com

The most provocative, astonishing, and frustrating database is Google Book Search. This is the Google project to digitize every book on the planet, starting with a handful of American research libraries. (They have recently announced plans to scan historical newspapers in a similar fashion.) One of those libraries happens to be University of Michigan, which has one of the best collections of Japanese books outside of Japan. The problem is that the database is riddled with mistakes and the OCR technology for Japanese seems to be rudimentary, which makes using it something of a roller coaster ride.

The main problem is that the books are divided into several categories. There are volumes available in full text, but these are primarily public domain works from before the age of cinema. Most items are available in "preview mode," which means you only get to see snippets of text. Others allow no searching or samples whatsoever. An impressive number of Japanese books and periodicals that have already been scanned, but unfortunately the vast majority of them fall into the last category. And while the OCR often garbles results, Google Book Search can already be used for trolling the archive. For example, a search for the great Nikkatsu action star Shishido Jō turns up 371 hits. Many of these are unusual and easy to miss. At the moment, one can basically use Google Book as a free-of-charge substitute for those without access to the primary Japanese databases.

That said, when it works it is astonishing. For an ideal hit, one can download the entire work or read enough in snippets to judge the reference's value; links send you to the book's WorldCat page to learn which libraries own a copy, or to online bookstores to buy the book, or even to *furuhon'ya* that stock it. For English-language works, there are sometimes lists of quotes from the book with links to other books that have used the very same quote—inviting a potentially endless dive into the archives. Google Book can also be extremely useful for browsing through the footnotes and bibliographies of monographs when casting a wide net for sources. In any case, the current shape of Google Book is remarkably rough, but it will undoubtedly be indispensable in the very near future.

IMDB (Internet Movie Database)
www.imdb.com

This began informally on the Usenet newsgroup rec.arts.movies in 1989, whose members turned it into a database in 1990. Amazon purchased it outright in 1998, and it is now the single largest database on cinema. There is a professional level that requires a subscription, but the information on Japanese talent and production companies is minimal. The information in the general database on Japanese film is weighted towards recent cinema, but is riddled with mistakes, aberrant transliterations, and omissions. Use only with care.

JFDB
j-pitch.jp/jfdb/
「日本映画データベース」

A new database that currently only covers films made after 2002, but since it comes in both Japanese and English versions, it can be quite helpful to those who don't read Japanese. Supported by UniJapan through its J-Pitch arm, which promotes networking between Japanese and foreign producers, it is primarily intended for industry people and even includes contact information. As with other industry-produced data, it is not always reliable with name readings, but many entries include photos, plot summaries, commentaries, festival awards, and official website links.

JMDB (Japan Movie Database)
www.jmdb.ne.jp
「日本映画データベース」

Modelled after the IMDB, this Japanese-language version lists 34,000 titles and 75,701 personal names as of 2001, and it covers the entire history of Japanese cinema. The product of a single individual, the JMDB has its pluses and minuses: it has mistakes, but sometimes more staff information than *KineJun;* it does not have plot summaries, but it gives technical information like release date and film length that *KineJun* does not have. More importantly, it includes the pre-1951 films *KineJun's* database does not cover. In most cases, the database repeats the credit information in *KineJun,* but in some cases, it avails itself of more detailed information printed elsewhere. Overall, an important resource. Unfortunately, few films after 2005 have been added, so the database is now virtually dormant.

KineJapan & Kinema Club
pears.lib.ohio-state.edu/Markus/Welcome.html

Few people realize that the entire backlog of online conversations from KineJapan, the newsgroup connected to the website and informal collective Kinema Club (159) is archived and searchable. The interface is extremely clunky, but it works (instructions are on the Kinema Club website). Most of the foreign scholars of Japanese cinema, and many Japanese scholars, have belonged to this newsgroup at one point. Their posts range from the informational to the speculative to the theoretical to the impressionistic. There are also quite valuable "reports from the field," descriptions of the reception context that usually are never committed to permanent media. Indeed, it is best to think of this as a new kind of scholarly publication for the digital age.

Another resource on the Kinema Club website is a bibliographic database. It contains over 1,500 entries, mostly periodical articles, in all the world's major languages. This was an early collaborative effort of Kinema Club; however, it certainly has lasting value, especially for the annotations.

Kinema junpō *zen eiga sakuhin dētabēsu*
www.walkerplus.com/movie/KineJun/
「キネマ旬報　全映画作品データベース」

Basically a database of *KineJun's* postwar (post-1951) film introductions (*shōkai*). The staff/cast information is rarely better than the JMDB, but it includes brief commentaries and plot summaries that, even if they are not always correct, are extremely useful. One can sometimes do content searches, but the search function on this database is poorly constructed. The name readings should be checked against another source before being used. Other online movie databases like Variety Japan and goo eiga use the same data.

Nichigai Database Service
www.nichigai.co.jp/database/index.html

This is probably the most important database for periodicals in Japan, featuring MagazinePlus. Unfortunately, it is subscription only, so most foreign libraries do not have it.

Nihon Eiga Shiryō no Kobeya
nihon-eiga.fan-site.net
「日本映画資料の小部屋」

Strictly speaking, this curious fan site is not a database, but the spirit certainly is. The site collects images of the covers for post-war runs of many periodicals, including the Big Three (120-122), fan oriented magazines, and PR organs for five studios. This makes it similar to the University of Iowa's Japanese Film Journal Table of Contents Browser (155). There is an inherent pleasure in scanning these covers and the orientation to cinematic pleasure they each imply; however, the site's real value is in the tables of contents that are also appended as images. The runs feature varying levels of completeness, and the inclusion of tables of contents are inconsistent (and sometimes easy to miss). On the other hand, there are so few searchable databases for Japanese film periodicals that this is a formidable research tool for performing spade work from afar.

Nii Scholarly and Academic Information Navigator (CiNii)
ci.nii.ac.jp

「Nii 論文情報ナビゲータ　国立情報学研究所」

This enormous database covers academic journals (including *Eizōgaku* [125] and *Eigagaku* [125]), university bulletins (*kiyō*), and quite a few film magazines (*Eiga hyōron*, *Kinema junpō*, among others).

Ōya Sōichi Library
www.oya-bunko.or.jp
「大宅壮一文庫」

It does not give the full text, but does the most complete job of indexing the strange and wonderful world of the popular press. The current web version covers the period after 1988. For earlier articles, you have to consult the printed version (81-82), which spans the Meiji up until 1995, or the CD-ROM version (158), which covers 1988-2007. If foreign Asia libraries don't have a subscription, they often have print or CD-ROM versions.

The Rest

.lain anime dētabāsu
lain.gr.jp/modules/mediadb
『.lain アニメデータベース』

Purely an anime database, and overwhelmingly weighted towards recent work.

allcinema ONLINE eiga dētabēsu
www.allcinema.net
『allcinemaONLINE映画データベース』

The cast/staff information differs little from *KineJun* or the IMDB, but this database sometimes includes original commentary, viewer comments, and video/DVD information. However, it is by no means inclusive and is weighted towards recent film.

Bibliography of Asian Studies
www.aasianst.org/bassub.htm

Offers comprehensive coverage of post-1971 periodicals on Asia in Western languages. For film periodicals, turn to the FIAF database above (150). Subscription required.

Japan Knowledge
www.japanknowledge.com
This is a complex set of databases and online resources (dictionaries, encyclopedias, *Imidas*, and a little bit of everything they could think of). Being able to search more than one name dictionary and encyclopedia is wonderful. Requires subscription.

Japanese Film Journal Table of Contents Browser
www.lib.uiowa.edu/eac/TOC/index.htm

This visual database at the University of Iowa contains scans of the following journals's tables of contents: *Eigagaku, Eiga geijutsu, Eiga kagaku kenkyū, Eizōgaku, Iconics,* and *Kinema junpō*. Not all the runs are complete, but if you are planning a visit to a library with these journals—or simply working interlibrary loan hard—this is a wonderful resource. Be sure to combine work on this site with a visit to *Nihon Eiga Shiryō no Kobeya.*

Japanese Horror Movies Database
www.fjmovie.com/horror

This is a delightful database of sci-fi and horror films. The database is searchable, but there are also indexes by personal name, title and keyword. A visit to the site is worth making, if only for the keywords list with its entries like Cannibalism, Living Statue, Strange Disease, and Transplantation of Organs. The credits are uneven and the site is replete with spelling and transliteration mistakes, but the poster art and DVD release information make up for these weaknesses.

National Diet Library Homepage
www.ndl.go.jp
「国立国会図書館」

The National Diet Library has a handful of rare books from early cinema in the Kindai Digital Library (search for words like *"eiga"* and *"katsudō shashin"*). Its Warp Database also archives a number of film festival websites and their iterations over the years.

NDL-OPAC
opac.ndl.go.jp

This is the main catalog for the National Diet Library, one of the most authoritative sources for Japanese book references.

Nichiei Archive
www.n-eigashinsha.jp
「日本映画新社　日映アーカイブ」

Nichiei's website has a database for *Nihon nyūsu, Asahi nyūsu,* the various local iterations of their newsreels, and other documenties in their catalog. The entries provide some nice data on each film and its content, as well as information on whether there is a video release for purchase. This all sounds nice, but in reality the database is rather difficult to use and produces unpredictable (and therefore probably unreliable) information. Nevertheless, it is certainly worth using before a visit to archives that hold the films, such as the Shōwa-kan (47-48), Kawasaki City Museum (14-15), or the National Film Center (23-25).

Nikkei Telecom21
telecom21.nikkei.co.jp
「日経テレコン21」

This is a package of databases based on Nihon Keizai Shinbun publications. Aside from full text searching of Nikkei's newspapers, it also has detailed economic profiles of companies.

Sakuhin dētabēsu: Anime, gēmu, manga, shōsetsu, dorama, tokusatsu, eiga
www.accessup.org/anime
「作品データベース　アニメ ゲーム 漫画 小説 ドラマ 特撮 映画」

A database of basically pop culture (or *otaku* culture?) texts.

Terebi dorama dētabēsu
www.qzc.co.jp/DRAMA
「テレビドラマデータベース」

A database of fictional television series and movies. The cast/staff and broadcast information are very helpful, but the database only occasionally includes explanatory comments.

NACSIS Webcat
webcat.nii.ac.jp/webcat.html

The Webcat database reveals where a given book may be found in Japanese research libraries. It is probably most useful for tracking down an unusual book or doctoral dissertation not held by one of the main film libraries in Japan.

Vivia
www.tv-asahipro.co.jp
「ヴィヴィア」

This is the website for TV Asahi Productions, which holds the archive for all the newsreels and films produced by *Asahi shinbun* and TV Asahi since the Russo-Japanese war. The database of the films they are marketing is a nice tool to use before contacting or visiting archives where you can actually see the films. TV Asahi is only interested in selling footage by the second, so outside of the Vivia database they are of little use to researchers.

Yomiuri Eizō
www.y-eizou.co.jp/contents/m_lib/m_lib_top.html
「読売映像」

Yomiuri shinbun started producing newsreels in 1937. This website has a set of pdf files that list the primary contents of the newsreels for a given year, a handy resource for visiting other archives. Yomiuri itself only sells clips at steep prices for broadcast and film production.

Discs

It's hard to get excited about CD-ROMs and DVD-ROMs now that everything is going conveniently online. We suspect this section will look increasingly quaint as the years ago by.

Kinema junpō *besuto ten & kōgyō dēta zenshi 1951-2005*
Tokyo: Kinema Junpōsha, 2005.
『キネマ旬報ベストテン&興行データ全史1951-2005』キネマ旬報社, 2005.

Kinema junpō consolidates a variety of their reference books on this DVD-ROM. The Best Ten lists are there for marketing purposes. Where this would be useful is for the data on films, festival awards, and especially the index of the magazine.

Masterpieces of Japanese Silent Cinema
Tokyo: Urban Connections, 1998.

Matsuda Film Productions (17-18), along with the company Urban

Connections, put together this bilingual DVD-ROM, which supplements the film data of the *Kinema junpō* disc above through its focus on the silent era. They include various levels of data on over 12,000 films, as well as some visual materials like stills and leaflets. What's best about this project is the way they drew on Matsuda's collection to digitize clips from 45 films. The quality is what you would expect for 1998, pixely and poor, but the clips are delightful and feature a wide variety of *benshi*, who are subtitled in English. For all of these reasons, we often introduce the art of the *benshi* to students by jumping quickly from clip to clip in the classroom. One drawback: they rather rudely restrict playback to Windows machines.

Ōya Sōichi Bunko zasshi kiji sakuin CD-ROM-ban
Tokyo: Kinokuniya Shoten, 1997-.
『大宅壮一文庫雑誌記事索引CD-ROM版』紀伊国屋書店, 1997-.

The first digitization of Ōya Sōichi Library's indexing of the popular press was accomplished on CD-ROM, and covers the years 1988 to 2007. They are only now converting that information to web-searchable database form. Many Asia libraries outside of Japan carry either these CD-ROMs or the printed version, even if they don't carry the ongoing subscription to the later web index. See p. 53 for more information.

Websites

There are literally hundreds, if not thousands of websites on or related to Japanese film. Like the net itself, they constitute a sea of information that often is more likely to drown you than provide you with solid grounding. But there are a number of secure islands out there with great information that can be of use to researchers.

These can be of many kinds, but we want to in particular single out the Center for Japanese Studies at the University of Michigan. By engaging in digital reprints of old publications they have been important in filling in the gaps in the archives, but without the cost imposed by the commercially produced reprints sold in Japan. The limited-run paper reprints usually cost many thousands of dollars; by way of contrast, UM's site is free, and even includes moving images. We can only hope we see more of such projects on the internet in the future.

Thanks to the protean nature of the Internet, any attempt to list online resources on paper is doomed to instant obsolescence. Luckily, should any of these sites disappear, some vestige can be recalled through the Internet Archive's Way Back Machine: www.archive.org.

Aozora bunko
www.aozora.gr.jp
「青空文庫鵜」

A large, online pot of public domain books, including the collected works of many authors. Access is free, it's capable of full-text searching, and output is either by text file or html. Unfortunately, there is no single subject heading for cinema, so one must either browse or search by name or keyword. There are important writings by the likes of Itami Mansaku, Terada Torahiko, Nakai Masakazu, Tosaka Jun, and a few others.

Cinema St.
www.cinema-st.com
「港町シナマ通り」

A fan site focusing on movie theaters, it has wonderful introductions to over 170 different kinds of cinema halls in Japan, from first run theaters to *meigaza*, from mini-theaters to pink movie houses.

Eiga Daisuki!
www.cinemanavi.co.jp
「映画大好き！」

This is the website of Kōgyō Tsūshinsha, one of the main sources for box office statistics. Their website is under construction and out-of-date, but does provide some recent data in English and Japanese. The very meaty data, such as daily grosses by screen, is only available by subscription or through the television shows and magazines that purchase their services.

Kinema Club and KineJapan
pears.lib.ohio-state.edu/Markus

Kinema Club is an informal organization of scholars and fans of Japanese cinema. It started as a group of young scholars copying and sharing magazine indexes, going online in 1995. The website is woefully out of date, although it does have useful sections such as a searchable, annotated bibliography of essays on Japanese film (with several thousand entries in English, German, French and other languages). Kinema Club has been more important for a series of workshops, which are documented in a special section. By way of contrast, their email newsgroup KineJapan is a lively forum on Japanese moving image media, thanks to over 600 members around the world. People often post research inquiries to the list, the archive of which is searchable. The website explains how to subscribe.

Japan Video Software Association
www.jva-net.or.jp
「日本映像ソフト協会」

Contains reports on video sales and rentals. Recent years are online; earlier data is available by request.

JaPop'90
web.tiscali.it/japop90

This Italian site provides a nicely organized collection of links, organized primarily by personal name. This makes it easy to navigate to pages that list homepages, filmographies, interviews, reviews and articles. There is also a good, multi-lingual list of online zines. As the name implies, the emphasis is on film from the 1990s and beyond.

Mark Schilling's Tokyo Ramen
japanesemovies.homestead.com

Mark Schilling is an industry journalist, critic, programmer, and excellent historian of Japanese cinema. His website collects many of his reviews, interviews and articles over the years.

Midnight Eye
www.midnighteye.com

This is the premiere online journal for Japanese film. Not only is the design sharp, but the content is wide-ranging, smart and well-written. The critics of *Midnight Eye* are devoted to everything Japanese cinema has to offer, from Kurosawa Akira to the pink film, prewar animation to video art. They review books new and old, and feature regular interviews with directors, actors, and craftspeople. The links section is fantastic, not least because it covers European languages other than English and is annotated. What's more, the site is searchable.

Motion Picture Producers Association of Japan, Inc. (Eiren)
www.eiren.org
「日本映画製作者連盟」

Borne out of the ruins of war in 1945, Eiren is the main association for the mainstream film industry. They have general box office data for the postwar era. The information becomes noticeably richer after 2000. The Eirin site also has what it calls the "official database" of films made and/or distributed by the four majors: Shōchiku, Tōhō, Tōei, and Kadokawa Eiga. It only covers films after 1970, but given its connections to the majors, includes films that have not yet been released.

Tangemania: Aaron Gerow's Japanese Cinema Page
www.aarongerow.com

This is Aaron's homepage. It contains links to much of his work, but the best part is his blog. It contains many "reports from the field," the field of Japanese film studies to be specific. Tangemania turns its attention to news, incidents, and events not covered by the other major blogs on Japanese film. This includes visits of filmmakers to university-sponsored events, as well as academic conferences. It is both thoughtfully analytical and breezily chatty in turns.

UM Center for Japanese Studies Electronic Reprint Series
www.umich.edu/~iinet/cjs/publications/cjsfaculty/filmseries.html

The University of Michigan's Center for Japanese Studies Publication Program has an online reprint series devoted to motion pictures. It publishes both out-of-print classics, like Noël Burch's *To the Distant Observer* and David Bordwell's *Ozu and the Poetics of Cinema,* and various archival materials. The latter includes a large collection of books, magazines, censorship records and even movies (in quicktime) from the prewar proletarian film movements.

UniJapan
www.unijapan.org

The Japan Association for International Promotion of the Moving Image, otherwise known as UniJapan, is a non-profit organization created through the film industry in 1957. They have strong ties to the Ministry of Economy, Trade and Industry (METI) and more recently the Tokyo International Film Festival. As a broker of information on the industry, they are a prime source of statistics on the (postwar) industry. The site is thoroughly bilingual, in English and Japanese.

Variety Asia Online
www.varietyasiaonline.com

Variety is the venerable industry rag for the American film industry, and as the Asian markets become increasingly important to Hollywood's bottom line they have become one of the best sources of regular information on the Japanese situation. This website collects a steady stream of stories about Asia and organizes them under various themes, one being "Japan." Unfortunately, both website and blog became "historical" in 2009 when the financial crisis forced *Variety* to close its Hong Kong office. For the time being all the previous content remains online.

Going to Japan? Be prepared! To see what's happening in theaters right now, check out the following websites:

Eigakan e ikō
www.eigakan.org
「映画館へ行こう」

Eiga seikatsu
www.eigaseikatu.com
「映画生活」

Movie Walker
www.walkerplus.com/tokyo/movie

Pia
www.pia.co.jp

VI. FAQ

How do I find 16mm and 35mm films for public programming?
Those in Japan are lucky to have archives to draw on. Markus helped crack the National Film Center's collection for public programming, when they agreed to supply prints to the Yamagata International Documentary Film Festival for a retrospective commemorating the 50th anniversary of Pearl Harbor. Now they collaborate with festivals and public programs across Japan, immeasurably enriching Japanese film culture. Many of the other Japanese archives listed in the first section lend films. In Tokyo, the Hibiya Public Library (39-40) lends out 16mm films, and the Hiroshima City Cinematographic and Audio-Visual Library (40) has a similar system.

For those outside of Japan, the NFC is no option, unless the sponsoring institution belongs to FIAF. On the other hand, some of the smaller archives regularly rent their films, most particularly Matsuda (17-18) and Planet (15-16). Each archive in the world has a different policy regarding public performances; you can always ask if they have a given film and if they're willing to rent it.

In the U.S. there are still a number of non-theatrical distributors hanging in there, despite the home video onslaught. However, the best resource for foreign events remains the Japan Foundation (59-60). See Chapter 2 for information on both.

How do I find 16mm and 35mm films for research?
Archives are increasingly allowing you to search their holdings on line, but it's a rare archive that actually shows you a complete list of their holdings. They simply have too many reels of questionable provenance. No archive wants to risk trouble with a copyright-holder. Thus, there are usually public and private lists. This means it is worth contacting an archivist directly and describing your project, or even better supplying a list of films you are searching for. Some are more welcoming to researchers, but nearly all are happy to help—as long as you strictly follow their rules and don't expect instant service.

Where can I find videos of a given film?
Check your library. If you don't find it there try interlibrary loan. A surprising number of libraries respond to requests for multimedia. If all else fails, you can purchase it through any number of websites. Good Japanese

websites include Amazon, Tsutaya, or Kinokuniya Bookweb. Or try English language sites that specialize in Asian videos like YesAsia.com or CDJapan. Most of these tend to have only DVDs in print or ones issued by major companies, although increasingly Amazon and other sites, including some of the used book sites, are selling used and out-of-print videos. Some used book stores, such as the big Book Off chain, also sell used DVDs.

For independent productions, you will often have to contact the company itself. This is worth trying because increasingly independent filmmakers are producing DVDs of their own works on their own computers. They are often happy to show their work to researchers, and are probably even happier if you offer to pay for it. To find out if a video or DVD has been commercially issued for a particular film, you can consult catalogs or filmographies like *Pia* or *Kinema junpō*. Some can be viewed at places we have listed.

Some may be tempted to buy a video from foreign websites that claim that international copyright law allows them to sell videos if they are not commercially available in that country. You should know that such excuses have no legal basis and thus that these videos are pirated and thoroughly illegal. Some may reason that they have to see the film for research and thus have to get it wherever they can, but remember that the more people buy pirated videos, the less money Japanese film companies and filmmakers make. Given how too many Japanese companies underestimate the market potential for old Japanese films, and thus put few out on DVD, frequenting pirate sites is only going to hamper the future availability of Japanese films. Buying a pirated version of a work a filmmaker herself is trying to sell is especially reprehensible. If you have to see a film but can't purchase it legally, carefully consult this guide for archives where you can see it, or use resources like KineJapan (152-153) to see if other scholars have personal copies you can borrow.

How do I find the contact information for a filmmaker or actor?

For actors, it is best to contact their agency using such talent lists as the Green Book (103) and the Red Book (107). Each issue of *Eiga nenkan* also prints the contact addresses of a limited number of directors, actors, and other film personnel. For directors it is possible to contact the Director's Guild of Japan, which represents over 200 filmmakers (3-2 5F Maruyama-chō, Shibuya, Tokyo 150-0044; Phone: 03-3461-4411; Fax: 03-3461-4457; www.dgj.or.jp; email: infom1@dgj.or.jp). Some of the biographical dictionaries in Chapter 4 also list contact information.

In some cases, these sources list home addresses. Whenever trying to contact a person, always make sure to follow the rules of etiquette and approach their office first. If you must contact them at home, do not suddenly phone them. Beware the time difference or you may be sending a fax to someone's bedroom in the middle of the night. In either case, it is best to write first, either by e-mail, fax or by snail mail.

Since the Green and Red books are held in few libraries, another possible source is the Pro version of the IMDB. However, in more cases than not, this simply refers you to the appropriate union. There are a few other directories for actors and singers; these are rarely in libraries, but one can usually find them at the film section of such big bookstores as Kinokuniya in Shinjuku.

How do I check the proper date of a film?

There are several ways of dating a film, the primary ones being the date of production, the date of release, and the date of copyright (especially if placed on the film itself). Many world archives prefer the last one, but since Japanese filmmakers only began to regularly include the copyright date on the film itself a couple decades ago, this method is useless in many cases. The date of production can be important at times, especially in cases like Kurosawa's *The Men Who Tread on the Tiger's Tail,* which was released seven years after it was shot. Even when you have a year of copyright, it can be important to know the release date, such as with recent independent films, which sometimes have to wait one or two years before getting an exhibition slot.

In general, most scholars of Japanese films use the release date to date a film, especially for works during the studio era, when the grand majority of films were released soon after they were produced. The best sources for obtaining the release date are the Kinema Junpōsha (95-97) or the Kagaku Shoin filmographies (94-95). The Japanese Movie Database (152) can help with a quick search, but as with other internet resources, it should be double checked before using its information in publication.

In the rare case that you are looking at an archival print missing all its credit information, one of the best clues is the manufacturer's code printed into the margin of the filmstrip. Most archives will have a key on hand, which will at least allow you to precisely date the production of the film stock itself.

Where can I catch a live benshi *performance?*

Since Matsuda Film Productions (17-18) programs most of these you can look up their upcoming performances on their website. They'll also help program an event as well, even if it's on the other side of the world. Many other outfits are showing silent films with *benshi,* so it is also worth consulting *Pia* (162) for a given region.

Where can I find the scenario for a film?

Those looking for scripts are in for some pleasant surprises. An unusual number of scripts have been published and through a wide variety of venues. There are journals devoted to scenarios, most notably *Shinario* (126-127). We list other journals and anthologies in the section above on script collections (111-115). Additionally, most of the major periodicals, including *Kinema junpō,* regularly publish scripts, although not as much as they used to.

The other pleasant surprise is Tanikawa Yoshio's *Shinario bunken* (111-112), which indexes most of the published scripts from the 1920s through the 1990s. No reference shelf is complete without this book, which is still in print (Yaguchi [66] keeps a stack on hand). Two other easy methods of tracking down scripts are Waseda's (28-29) card catalog for scripts and the online database at the Kawakita website (12-13).

When one enters a movie theater, from those of the major chains to the mini-theaters, there are almost always programs and books on sale; these sometimes have some version of the scenario inside. There is a growing collection of these programs at Yale's Sterling Library (53). There are inevitably piles of them in the used bookstores, but a few specialty stores like @Wonder (63) and Vintage organize them for easy searching. Online *furuhon'ya* are also starting to offer programs, making these programs even more accessible. For independent films, it's not unusual for producers to publish a book of essays on their film; these books often include the script. To track them down, search WorldCat for the title of the film.

We should point out that most of the scenarios described above are edited for publication, so care must be taken in making claims based on them (for example, citing a difference between script and finished film). Researchers must always note the version they are looking at. There are early drafts (usually numbered or dated), the official production script (which is usually printed and bound), one or more post-production scripts (some which include time-code while stripping commentary and screen direction), dialogue scripts produced for foreign translators (which may be found at a surprising number of archives in Europe and North America), and then the scenarios edited for public consumption with their multitude of approaches. Unfortunately, the scripts you find in periodicals often neglect to indicate which version they are publishing and whether or not it has been revised.

Obviously, the most useful and potentially enlightening scripts are the preproduction and production scripts, especially when their provenence can be assertained. For example, the Museum of Kyoto Film Library Centre (18-19) has a significant collection of Itō Daisuke and Yamanaka Sadao scripts with the director's own marginalia. On the other end of the production process are the dubbing scripts for foreign works; Waseda has the personal collection of star *seiyū* Wakayama Genzō, with upwards of 9,000 scripts. We note other significant collections of directors and screenwriters in Chapter 1. Nevertheless, the first stops for a production script search should be the National Film Center (23-25) and Waseda's Tsubouchi Theater Museum (28-29), which have 30,000 and 25,000 titles respectively. Another approach is to search by studio: for Shōchiku go to the Ōtani Library (27-28) and for Tōei inquire at Movieland (55-56); both have relatively complete scenario collections of their respective studio's output. The Setagaya Literary Museum (26-27) also has thousands of Tōhō scripts.

There is one other genre of script: the censorship scenario. These are very hard to come across, with one exception. The Prange Collection (10-12) contains the scenarios for all films made during the Occupation. They are often translated into English and accompanied by paperwork produced in the censorship process. See Kyōko Hirano's *Mr. Smith Goes to Tokyo* for a provocative use of this collection. Unfortunately, these are not included in the microfiche set, so one must travel to Maryland to use them. In the prewar era, censorship laws required the submission of enface scenarios of foreign films undergoing translation, and are an unusual resource for studying the prewar reception context for foreign films. A smattering of these can be found in all the major archives, especially Kawakita (12-13), the National Film Center (23-25) and Columbia University (8-9).

How can I find programs and other ephemera about a given film?
Film programs and handbills are an important part of Japanese film exhibition culture and can also be a great resource for scholars studying a particular film. Those for classics can run into the hundreds of dollars, but most postwar programs are surprisingly inexpensive. Handbills serve as advertising and are found in the lobby of most theaters and programs are first sold at the theater itself. These, as well as other ephemera such as pressbooks (which are only given out at press screenings or some preview screenings), preview cards, posters, and lobby cards, do find their way into the used book market. The major used film book stores like Isseidō and Yaguchi Shoten sell some pamphlets and other ephemera, but stores like @Wonder and Vintage really specialize in such materials. You can also find them on internet used book stores or even on Yahoo Auctions in Japan.

If you merely want to look at these ephemera for research purposes, the main institutions like Waseda (28-29), the Film Center (23-25), Kawakita (12-13), Ōtani Library (27-28), and Tōei Movieland (55-56) are the place to go in Japan. Both Waseda and the Film Center have significant collections of old theater programs (before they started centralizing program production by making one pamphlet for one film for the entire country), which can be prohibitively expensive on the used market. The Yale University Library is currently assembling a collection of programs, handbills and pressbooks, but it is weighted towards the last two decades.

I need stills for my book; where can I buy them?
You can try to purchase them at used book stores, especially stores that specialize in ephemera like @Wonder and Vintage, or which deal with certain genres like porno. "Bromides" or star portraits are still sold at shops like Marubell in Asakusa (68-69). Whether you find what you want is a matter of luck, but even if you do manage to buy what you want, that does not necessarily give you the right to use them. Japanese companies in recent years have gotten strict about the use of stills, sometimes excessively so. Many of the big companies allow free use of them only during the time the

film is in first-run theaters, and demand a usage fee after that. Up until only a few years ago, institutions like the Kawakita Memorial Film Institute used to readily provide copies of stills for publication, but now they refrain from doing that except for films quite clearly in the public domain. That should technically be stills for films older than 50 years, but most archives will balk at giving you a still from a film even older than that if the company is still in existence. You will need to get copyright clearance, and unfortunately the major companies will demand a significant fee. Independent film producers and distributors are much more reasonable, so don't hesitate to contact them. International copyright law considers frame blow-ups the equivalent of a textual quote of a larger work, so they should be publishable without clearance. Japanese courts have also established, for instance, that use of panels from a published manga in a research book is in most cases a legitimate quotation and can be done without permission. This should cover the use of frame grabs as well.

The main sources for stills in Japan other than the original production company are the National Film Center (23-25), the Kawakita Memorial Film Institute (12-13), Tōei Movieland (55-56) and Matsuda (17-18). Outside of Japan, you can try these sources:

Photofest
32 East 31 St., 5th floor
New York, NY 10016 U.S.A.
Phone: 212-633-6330

The New York Public Library for the Performing Arts
40 Lincoln Center Plaza
New York, NY 10023-7498 U.S.A.
Phone: 212-870-1630

Margaret Herrick Library
Academy Film Archive
Center for Motion Picture Study
333 South La Cienega Boulevard
Beverly Hills, CA 90211 U.S.A.
Phone: 310-247-3020
Special collections: 310-247-3000

The British Film Institute
Stills, Posters and Designs
21 Stephen Street
London W1T 1LN U.K.
Phone: 020-7957-4797
Fax: 020-7323-9260

At the time of writing, the MoMA stills archive was closed and unavailable for use. If and when that gets running again, it can be another source. Another potential source is the Harvard Film Archive, which purchased a German collection of 1,000,000 stills in 2008. The number of Japanese films represented had yet to be determined at the time of writing, but the university library does have plans to digitize the collection so visit their website for more information.

Where do I find box office data?

Japanese companies had long been rather secretive about box office data, in part because they didn't want people to know of their failures, but also because they resisted transparency in business practice. In fact up until 1999, distributors only publicized distribution income (*haishū*), not box office gross, thus keeping the theater take secret. (Since *haishū* tends to be 40-60% of total box office, you can still estimate the total if you know the *haishū* figure.) Especially in the days of *maeuri* ticket movies (where advanced tickets were aggressively sold but not always used at the theater), box office accounting was not always kosher. Even now that total box office is reported, it is only for the major successes of the year, leaving the scholar with few avenues for getting precise business information for lower ranking films. Weekly rankings seen on sites like Yahoo Japan only give the order of the films, with no monetary amounts (you are better off looking in *Variety* for that).

The Motion Picture Producers Association of Japan (Eiren: www.eiren.org) releases the official business results for the industry each year, including box office for the top 20 or 30 films. This report is available on the web, or in publications like *Kinema junpō* or *Eiga nenkan*. *Kinema junpō*'s February 15 issue (*gejungō*) may also include figures for the top single-theater films (*tankan rōdoshō*). Specialty trade sheets like *Kōgyō tsūshin* also provide precise information for their subscribers about the results of a variety of films at a set of specific theaters, which is usually enough to judge whether a movie was a hit or not. The business columns in *Kinema junpō* can also provide more specific figures on a film's opening, as well as estimates on how well it will do (which sometimes may be the only figure you can get). Also check out business related books and reports, such as government white papers or trade organization reports (some of which can be downloaded from ministry or organization websites), since they can provide not only general industry statistics, but also occasional survey results and case studies. You might be lucky and find your film was put under the looking glass.

Otherwise you just have to scour out newspaper articles and interviews to find if someone blurted out the information everyone was keeping secret. As with many other aspects of Japanese film studies, hard work is often necessary.

How do I figure out transliterations for Japanese names?
Obtaining accurate readings of Japanese names is one of the banes of Japan studies abroad. Even names that you think might be obvious may be subject to aberrant readings, so you have to check. The difficulties are multiplied with a discipline like film studies that has not enjoyed the official support, either governmental or academic, necessary for the publication of comprehensive and thorough name dictionaries. Another, more recent problem is the proliferation of internet databases and records that utilize a variety of often arbitrary and unofficial transliteration systems. While the user-participation method of some of these sources can be a plus at times, at other times it creates as many transliteration systems as there are users. Some treat the keyboard shortcuts for inputting Japanese on their computer as official romanization, others wrongly assume that English sounding names like Jōji or Mari should be rendered "George" or "Mary," and still others treat conveniences like "Itami Juuzou," utilized by those who want to be accurate about pronunciation but cannot input macrons in e-mail or HTML, as what should be used in print. Recently Japanese distribution companies have been submitting credit information themselves to databases like the IMDB, but in some cases these are prepared by part-time employees who have not checked with everyone involved in the film about name readings, or who use obscure romanization systems like *kunrei*, which Japanese learn at school, but is almost never used abroad and not even in the majority of situations at home. Even if they do check with an individual about rendering their name in English, that person may make up some odd Anglicization without knowing that the majority of foreign databases have already recorded their names according to official romanization rules. The result of all this is confusion and chaos, with some online databases featuring separate records of two or three actors who actually are actually the same person.

It is thus incumbent upon, if not also the responsibility of the Japanese film scholar to both check multiple and reliable sources for accurate name readings as well as consistently use official romanization, which at least in English, is modified Hepburn. One of the most embarrassing things you can do is get names wrong. So which sources are best for obtaining accurate name readings? As with the United States, it is the national library—in this case, the National Diet Library—that serves as the primary authority on name readings. Thus, the first place to check is the NDL or LOC, or similarly authoritative library catalogs (Iowa, Columbia, Yale, Harvard, Michigan, Waseda, the National Film Center, etc.). On the net, one can use Webcat or WorldCat, but be wary that both also contain records created by lesser libraries that did not follow the rules or thoroughly check name authority records. The other disadvantage with the NDL is that it only gives readings of those who are authors, which for a film usually means just the director and the screenwriter; other personnel are only listed if they authored a book or other material. For book authors, be sure to check the copyright page in back; it often renders the author's name in *romaji* or *rubi.*

In many cases, then, one should consult film-specific name dictionaries like those listed in Chapter 4 (102-109). There are more general *jinmei jiten* available, but most of those just refer you back to the film-specific ones. The Kinema Junpōsha dictionaries are usually the first place to start, but since it and the NDL can contain mistakes, it is always best when preparing something for publication to confirm those readings through other major sources like the *Sekai eiga daijiten* (88) and the Kagaku Shoin and Nichigai Asoshiētsu dictionaries. Those can also provide name readings of figures other than directors and actors. If you still cannot find a name reading, as can often be the case with prewar film personnel or those who worked in marginal sectors like documentary, you probably will have to check existing publications to see if anyone has romanized the name before. If all that fails, you'll have to come up with a reading yourself. P.G. O'Neill's or Niwa Motoji's dictionaries are good at providing possible readings or personal or family names, but it is sometimes good to check with databases like Webcat to see which readings are more popular and thus more likely.

Does any website have a good collection of internet links?

As with anything online, this information is likely to change. One good resource is *Midnight Eye*. It collects links for directors, studios, actors, film schools, and zines in English, German, French, Spanish and Italian. Annotations make the site all the more useful. An even more impressive site is JaPop'90; it is in Italian, but is easy to navigate to many hundreds of websites, online interviews and reviews.

Indexes

For convenience of searching, we have provided five indexes covering personal names, subjects, titles (of books, films, etc.), electronic resources, and names of institutions that appear in this book. The indexes are generally exclusive, with only a few headings being shared. Place-names are included in the subject index. Numbers in italics indicate major entries or sections on the topic in the book.

These indexes are meant not only to serve as a guide to the persons, institutions, publications, and issues mentioned in this book, but also to help researchers find an institution or a publication that may cover the subject they are studying or contain the item they might need. It can thus give directions according to your topic, be it a person, studio, place, or other such subject. One could thus look under Itō Daisuke and find out about not only the published collection of his scenarios, but also where his personal papers are located. The indexes focus on what is actually mentioned in the text, so just because a library is not indexed here for a category does not mean that library does not contain such materials. One can assume, for instance, that major collections such as Waseda and the Film Center have examples of most everything. These indexes are thus intended only as a preliminary guide; you'll still often have to do a lot of footwork on your own. But if you find any secret caches of stuff or information you think we should list, let us know.

Name Index

Subject Index

Title Index

Electronic Resources Index

Institution Index

ABOUT THE AUTHORS

Abé Mark Nornes is Professor of Asian Cinema at the University of Michigan, where he specializes in Japanese film and documentary. He is the author of *Cinema Babel: Translating Global Cinema*, a theoretical and historical look at the role of translation in film history. He has also written two books on nonfiction film in Japan: *Forest of Pressure: Ogawa Shinsuke and Postwar Japanese Documentary* and *Japanese Documentary Film: From the Meiji Era to Hiroshima* (all from the University of Minnesota Press).

Aaron Gerow is Assistant Professor of Japanese Cinema at Yale University. He has published widely in a variety of languages on early, wartime, and recent Japanese film, and is author of *Kitano Takeshi* (BFI) and *A Page of Madness: Cinema and Modernity in 1920s Japan* (Center for Japanese Studies, The University of Michigan). He has a book on Japanese film culture of the 1910s forthcoming from the University of California Press.